The THREE QUESTIONS

Prosperity and the Public Good

BOB RAE

VIKING

VIKING
Published by the Penguin Group
Penguin Books Canada Ltd, 10 Alcorn Avenue, Toronto, Ontario,
Canada M4V 3B2
Penguin Books Ltd, 27 Wrights Lane, London w8 5tz, England
Penguin Putnam Inc., 375 Hudson Street, New York, New York
10014, U.S.A.
Penguin Books Australia Ltd, Ringwood, Victoria, Australia
Penguin Books (NZ) Ltd, cnr Rosedale and Airborne Roads, Albany
Auckland 1310, New Zealand

Penguin Books Ltd Registered Offices: Harmondsworth, Middlesex,
England

First published 1998
10 9 8 7 6 5 4 3 2 1

Printed and bound in Canada on acid free paper ⊛

CANADIAN CATALOGUING IN PUBLICATION DATA

Rae, Bob, 1948–
    The three questions: prosperity and the public good

ISBN 0-670-87824-3

1. Canada– Politics and government – 1993– .* 2. Canada –
Economic conditions – 1991– . 3. Social policy – Canada. I. Title.

FC635.R33 1998   971.064'8   C98-931373-5
F1034.2.R33 1998

Visit Penguin Canada's website at www.penguin.ca

For Arlene, Judith, Lisa and Eleanor
— "let me count the ways"

CONTENTS

From Protest to Power was a personal memoir of twenty years in active politics. As I grow older, I have had to discard some ideas and policies because they no longer make sense. This strikes me as entirely healthy. I would invite others to do the same.

No doubt some will see in these pages the sure signs of the impact of the "capitalist embrace." A balanced reading will show no such thing. For many years my life was in politics, most of them as the leader of the Ontario New Democrat Party. I have spent the last three years as a lawyer in a Canadian-based international law firm. I also teach at the University of Toronto, and serve as a director on the boards of a number of companies and non-profit organizations.

My perspectives have no doubt broadened, but my commitments have not changed. I have never believed that the choice between economic prosperity and social justice was a simple either/or proposition. This book is an argument on the need for both.

Some of the ideas in this book have been tried out as lectures and talks I have given in the past few years. At the University of Toronto I have had the good fortune to teach undergraduate and graduate students in history, industrial relations, political science and law. Massey College, its Master, John Fraser, and its students and fellows have encouraged me, for which I am grateful.

The students of the universities of Guelph, Windsor, Carleton, Western, Queen's, Royal Military College, Simon Fraser, Regina, Concordia, McGill and St. Francis Xavier have heard some of these ideas as well, and I express my deep gratitude to them all for their hard questions and comments.

In particular, Chapter 7 is based on the Mallory Lecture I gave at McGill University in 1997. Chapter 8 is a distillation of the Winegard Lecture I gave at the University of Guelph and the Allan J. MacEachen Lectures at Saint Francis Xavier University in 1996 and 1997. My views on education in Chapter 6 have also appeared in Policy magazine. Certain arguments have also been aired in *The Globe and Mail*, and I thank that newspaper for allowing me to repeat them here.

My partners, associates, and friends at Goodman

Phillips & Vineberg have made a point of letting me pursue an eclectic practice. I am grateful for their fellowship and support. My partner Michael Levine is also my agent. His support has always made a difference. I also owe much to Eddie Goodman, whose wit, energy and loyalty to friends more than compensates for an occasionally errant political judgment.

Karen Golden, an articling student at the time, was extremely helpful in gathering information and analysis on charitable contributions, Hillel, and Edmund Burke. My good friends David Mackenzie and Peter Warrian read an earlier version of the manuscript and made many comments and criticisms. The mistakes that remain are of course my responsibility alone.

My editors, Cynthia Good and Mary Adachi, made me rewrite and revise. I may have been grumpy at the time, but I am grateful now. Sonia Zanardi deciphered an array of changes in scribbled handwriting and e-mails with patience and, more important, humour.

My wife, Arlene, and our children, Judith, Lisa, and Eleanor, have surrounded me with love and support. In this project, as in all others, they have also come with advice. For all this I am eternally grateful.

Toronto and Portland
July, 1998

The THREE QUESTIONS

The Rabbi's
Three Questions

CHANGE IS THE CLICHÉ OF OUR TIME. IT ALSO happens to be a prevailing truth. Walter Lippmann once described public opinion as "the pictures in our heads." Marshall McLuhan pointed out that we spend our lives viewing much of life "through a rear view mirror." Most of us continue to think about our private hopes and public lives with images that do not reflect current reality, let alone future possibilities.

The baby boom generation, of which I am very much a part, grew up with certain key assumptions. Canada, we thought, had a national economy with a resource base that seemed unlimited and strong manufacturing that would be made even stronger with the intervention and leadership of the federal government.

Social programmes would continue to expand with rising real incomes. The gap between rich and poor would naturally grow more narrow. Sitting around in the college cafeteria with my fellow students in the late 1960s, we were not confronted with the now-perennial "Will there be a job for me?" As in cafeteria food, the choices were many, but they were not all appetizing by any means. However, today's angst is very different. Even sex has changed. We worried about pregnancy. Our children worry about the possibility of disease and death.

The world of the 1950s and 1960s was one where a typical family had two parents and one wage-earner. Dad worked and mom stayed home with the kids. Many policy makers still carry that picture in their heads; many politicians still launch an appeal to that mythical family. Yet we know that the reality is very different. One-parent families are common, not exceptional. Women have entered the workforce and are there to stay. Gays and lesbians rightfully expect their partnerships to be recognized by law and custom.

If the world at home has been transformed, the world at work has changed dramatically as well. Canada's economy is at once more local and more global. We are more dependent on trade than ever before. National governments seem less capable of responding to our needs and demands. The digital economy gives rise to new opportunities, but the technological revolution is even more bewildering and dramatic than the industrial changes that shaped our past. Patterns of work have changed, and will continue to do so: more people work part-time, while hours of work for many others have increased dramatically.

The well-paid male industrial or resource worker who alone could provide for his family is no longer at the centre of our national economy. There is a sense that the reassuring middle of our lives has been chipped away, with both success and failure counting for more. Incomes are becoming less, not more, equal.

Canada is now a multiracial country and in the next century will become even more so. The picture in many heads of Canada's aboriginal population is still of a group of people marginal to the mainstream, living in remote communities. In twenty years, the majority of the population in the inner core of some of our cities will be native people. In others the majority already speaks languages other than English or French. Many Canadians are having difficulty coming to terms with these realities.

The social democratic movement in Canada, of which I have been a member all my adult life, is also curiously uncertain in confronting these changes and conflicts. A set of policies—bigger centralized government, higher taxes, more intervention, and public ownership—have been challenged in virtually every social democratic party in the Western world. They cannot really be what social democracy is about, because they are not palatable recipes for governing.

The neo-conservative right, in the name of globalization and many other so-called "objective factors,"
has embraced inequality, the rising gap between rich
and poor, and the dismantling of the state as critical
steps along the one true way. There is a spirit of
ideological fervour at work greater than anything
seen on the left in recent memory. Tom Lehrer once
joked that the right won all the battles but "the left
had all the best songs." Now the right has the pas-
sion as well, as misplaced as it may be. If the neo-cons
have their way, there will be little trust and community left once they have done with their revolution.

Surrounding all this is the question of Canada
itself. The Quebec nationalists' rear-view perspective
is overwhelming. It is even celebrated on licence
plates: *"Je me souviens."* Remembered or imagined
grievance is the emotional life-force of a nationalism
that seems incapable of learning from other people's
excesses and mistakes. Yet Quebec sovereignists are
not alone in their determination to see life through a
single, backward lens: too many Canadians fail to see
federalism for the flexible, humane, and generous philosophy that it is. Too many are determined to force
the rest of us into a narrow, one-dimensional definition of the country and its identity. Nothing could be
less helpful.

The philosopher David Hume, who was known in
the eighteenth century as "le bon David," pointed out
the dangerous fallacy of shifting from what *is* to what
ought to be. Even the wisdom found on ashtrays tells

us to distinguish between accepting what can and cannot be changed. There are forces at work in our world, as there have always been, that are fundamentally technological in their origin, or that pertain to broader, impersonal forces. Some are summed up in the phrase "globalization."

As individuals, and in our political communities, the fact that we cannot stop all these changes should not be an excuse for giving up, or for simply becoming a cheerleader for the corporate agenda. We can strengthen our capacity both individually and together to cope with the impact of change. Social democracy goes astray when it pretends that politics and governments can do very much to stop technological change and innovation. At the same time, many on the right confuse the "is" of globalization with the "ought" of simply accepting all its effects. They preach a political quietism that is really just a cloak for greed.

The core value of social democracy—the sense that communities and equal citizenship matter, that ordinary people need to work together to improve their lives, to increase their ability to cope with the impact of change—is a good value. It is the "ought" that gives us the vision to face a difficult world.

The value is deep and enduring, but the policy instruments we choose to express it must change and evolve in response to experience. Some people (fortunately their numbers and influence are dwindling) get so attached to a nostrum—government ownership, a particular method of regulation, one system of taxation or another—that they fail to see that these policies are just tools. They are not the idea of social democracy itself. The essence of social democracy is its belief in the equal right of every person to enjoy the good things of life, its commitment to freedom, and its recognition of the enduring value of human solidarity. This is the spirit that fuelled Western farmers in the Depression and industrial workers who sought shorter hours and higher pay. From Tommy Douglas to Martin Luther King to Tony Blair, the fire is about everyone having that chance. The intuition behind the idea is the sense that elites take care of themselves, and that the "comfortable majority" looks to itself first. A decent politics understands that the public forum is the one place this imbalance of power and opportunity can be corrected.

More than a hundred and fifty years ago, a mayor of Toronto, political radical and exile William Lyon Mackenzie, expressed the idea this way:

> This then is politics. That part of our duty which teaches us to study the welfare of our whole country, and not to rest satisfied altho' our own household is well off when our neighbours are in difficulty and danger. The honest politician is he who gives all he can and means to promote the public good, whose charity begins at home *but does not end there.* The man who says he is no politician is either ignorant of what he is saying, or a contemptible selfish creature,

unworthy of the country or community of which he is a part.[1]

The scapegoating of today's political class in the current right-wing populist mood is easy and convenient. A passive public can blame someone else for their problems. Mackenzie's point is that, like it or not, "we are all politicians."

The argument of this book follows the famous three questions attributed to Rabbi Hillel, who lived in Babylon more than two thousand years ago: "If I am not for myself, who is for me? But if I am only for myself, what am I? And if not now, when?" The first question points to the enduring value of self-interest, which we ignore at our peril; the second to the need for generosity in a world that values greed too much; the third speaks to the need for action and the danger of doing nothing, a vice to which we are all, in our private and public moments, too prone.

The pursuit of self-interest in the economy is as natural for the trade unionist as it is for the entrepreneur or even tycoon. The healthy competition of the market, the achievement of our own individual success is not to be scorned or feared. Economic and political systems that do not attach a priority to the satisfaction of this demand from individuals have failed and will continue to fail. Prosperity matters. Billie Holiday reminded the world that "I have been poor and I have been rich, and rich is better."

This expression of the self is not just economic. It

is about who we are: sexually, culturally, politically. A bewildered Abraham turns to the heavens and says three words: "Here I am." They are potent words, and have been spoken by every person and every people seeking freedom. The assertion of identity is not self-indulgence. It is basic to our understanding of what it means to be human.

But it is not enough, which is why Hillel asked his second question: But if I am only for myself, what am I? The trouble with brash neo-conservatives, excessive nationalists, and single-issue politicians alike is that they all stop with the assertion of self-interest. Their obsession with self keeps them from coming to terms with the second question.

My views about the economy and government are really an extended discussion of the connection between Hillel's first two questions, about the relationship between prosperity and the public good.

Many on the right are trapped by arguments that the pursuit of self-enrichment by itself produces the best of all worlds. Many on the left fail to see that the modern economy can't simply be described as a universe of great evil.

Hillel's questions would lead to a more balanced view. A politics that ignores self-interest deserves to fail. An economics that ignores our common interest as citizens in the well-being of the broader community will eventually face a wall of public hostility. The poet Oliver Goldsmith wrote at the beginning of the industrial revolution of a world where "wealth accumulates and men decay."

While the public good is partly pursued by accepting the appetite for gain, gain alone is not enough. People will not accept being treated as commodities. They will insist on being recognized as citizens, members of families, cultures, and broader communities. They will insist on their rights.

We live in an age that celebrates claims. Hillel's second question suggests that we need to go beyond the pursuit of self-interest to an understanding of the responsibilities we have for other people. We live in a time of extraordinary technological change and financial windfall. Yet schools are underfunded and public goods are reviled by the business press.

As William Lyon Mackenzie put it, "charity begins at home but does not end there." It is a sign of health when we take responsibility for ourselves. The community and state overstep their bounds when they assume they know better than ourselves what is in our interest and what is "best" for us. It is equally discouraging when people point fingers at everyone but themselves for their fate.

But there is something very wrong when some companies assume no responsibility for environmental damage, or for the underfunding of the key social programmes that in fact train their workforces and provide support for their consumers. Many are reluctant citizens, pretending that the homeless around them are someone else's problem and responsibility alone.

Hillel's second question points to an ethic of shared responsibility. The third question reminds us we can't put these choices off forever.

Much as we might like, none of us can avoid these questions. They will not always lead to the same answers or conclusions. It would be a dull world if they did.

The First Question: Self-Interest and Prosperity

SELF-INTEREST, TECHNOLOGY, GLOBALIZATION. In some circles these are the fatal trinity of the corporate agenda. Yet it is hard to know how we can be part of the modern world without accepting their importance and even their value. None are absolutes. But each helps to define the world in which more and more people live.

More than thirty years ago the Canadian philosopher George Grant took the defeat of John Diefenbaker as a metaphor for the destruction of Canadian sovereignty itself. In *Lament for a Nation*, Grant wrote:

> To be a Canadian was to build, along with the
> French, a more ordered and stable society than the

> liberal experiment in the United States. Now that
> this hope has been extinguished, we are too old to be
> retained by a new master. We find ourselves like fish
> left on the shores of a drying lake.[1]

The premise of Grant's profound pessimism was that a ruthless technocratic civilization, whose heart was American capitalism itself, had captured the Canadian soul. Diefenbaker's nationalism, however wildly confused and contradictory, at least tried to throw a wrench into the imperial machine. That had failed, and with that failure the Canadian Experiment was over. Hence the lament.

Grant's book—and his other writings—have had a large following. Nationalism, and collectivism of a democratic kind were good. Continentalism and the individual pursuit of pleasure and profit were bad:

> In the mass era, most human beings are defined in
> terms of their capacity to consume. All other differences between them, like political traditions, begin to
> appear unreal and unprogressive. As consumption
> becomes primary, the border appears an anachronism, and a frustrating one at that.[2]

I have come to share neither George Grant's religious certainty nor his dismissal of pragmatism. His lament would no doubt be even stronger today. For the evil of "continentalism," we would now use the term "globalization." The argument is the same: what is unique and particular about Canada is being obliterated by impersonal corporate forces that know neither kindness nor loyalty.

This debate, of course, transcends Canada. No doubt George Grant has his alter ego in virtually every country in the world. As a student in England in the 1970s I watched with fascination as the British political community debated entry into the European Common Market. The arguments were remarkably parallel: competition would destroy British industry, Parliament would become irrelevant, sovereignty would be transferred to a corporate clique in Brussels, nothing good or positive would result. On the other side of the debate were those who saw an opportunity in larger markets and a more open Europe. Citizenship would be broadened, not limited. Little England could not survive.

For all the pain of adjustment, it is hard now to deny the positive benefits of the European experience for Britain. Margaret Thatcher's rule ended not because of her denial of trade union rights, her assault on the welfare state, or even the infamous poll tax: it was her anachronistic position on Europe.

Britain's entry into Europe coincided with the harsher effects of the Thatcher revolution. Yet the British labour movement did not object to Europe, once the price had been paid. Indeed the political effort by the left in Britain in the 1980s and 1990s was to use the Common Market as an argument for more progressive social policies. The rest of the

Thatcherite agenda was bitterly, if ineffectively, resisted. We are faced now with the final irony that the election of Tony Blair was marked by the wholesale acceptance of much of the Thatcher inheritance.

We have our own ironies at home. Jean Chrétien benefited from the deep opposition to the impacts of free trade, the GST, and fiscal restraint in his election in 1993. He has now become the chief advocate of all three; Brian Mulroney's loyal successor.

A conventional view would be to decry Blair and Chrétien as the apostles of the new corporatism, right-wing sell-outs who have abandoned the "people's agenda" for the big-business agenda of open markets, free trade, and private profit.

This misses a fundamental shift in the spirit of the age. Self-interest has a purpose and place at the heart of civil society. The pursuit of individual pleasure and profit are despised at our peril. A public philosophy which fails to understand the logic of Rabbi Hillel's first question—"If I am not for myself, who is for me?"—is bound to fail.

Appeals to self-sacrifice, compassion, and even generosity are rarely a successful substitute for appeals to self-interest. They are a necessary addition to it, as we shall see, but never a substitute.

Examples abound. The Democratic Party became a party of almost permanent opposition in the United States after the demise of Lyndon Johnson, because the liberalism of the 1960s was based on an assumption of ever-growing prosperity. As the economy grew more slowly in the years of stagflation, those with jobs resented more and more those who had none. For some, the politics of race and welfare were marked by a particular meanness and even selfishness. This misses the simple point that people view with alarm any reduction in their standard of living and sense of opportunity for themselves and their families. This is not "right wing." It is about as close to a fundamental part of human nature as you can get.

The premise of the market economy is the same as set out by John Locke, Adam Smith, and the classical economists: people pursue work out of necessity.

> We ought to look on it as a mark of goodness in God that he has put us in this life under a necessity of labour: not only to keep mankind from the mischiefs that ill men at leisure are very apt to do; but it is a benefit even to the good and the virtuous, which are thereby preserved from the ills of idleness.[3]

Most of us see it as a mark of civilized society that women and men are given a chance to work, to express themselves through their labour, to lead private lives that are marked by civility and mutual respect.

A politics that rejects this premise of individual economic rights will fail and deserves to fail. This lesson is being learned in every country in the world. In China, Deng Xiao Ping understood this when he made agricultural reform the basis of the end of the collectivist premises of Mao's thought and practice. The collectivism of Soviet agriculture in the 1930s, and China's so-called Great Leap Forward, we now know, were accompanied by brutality and mass starvation on a scale that is unimaginable. Tens of millions died in the name of collective sacrifice.

The central lessons in political economy of the twentieth century are twofold: first, the surest way to economic growth is through an essentially privately owned, entrepreneurially driven, market economy; second, the achievement of this economy and its broad acceptability require sound public policy, strong and capable governments, good governance, and a respect for the key institutions and principles of civil society.

The logic of economic development itself is behind the force and pace of globalization. Barring the disasters of political folly and the unpredictability of nature itself, we can only anticipate that this relentless pace will continue. Globalization is neither a demon nor a god. It is simply the economic reality of our time. Markets are becoming at once more international and locally intense.

What do I mean by "locally intense"? Growth *within* local and regional economies becomes more important, just as does wider trade around the world. No economies are self-sufficient; and fewer economies are principally national in scope. When the mayor of Shanghai and the premier of Ontario meet, they understand each other instantly, regardless of language or political barriers. They are both seeking to attract global investment and the advantages of technological transfer. They both will focus on education and how to build the public infrastructure necessary for growth. They both complain about national bureaucracies that don't understand the need for flexibility and innovation.

Cross-border capital flow around the world doubled between 1991 and 1995 to $1,258 billion. Foreign direct investment went up 1,000 per cent between 1986 and 1996. The world's stock of liquid financial assets, which was estimated at $11 trillion in 1980, is expected to exceed $100 trillion in 2000.

The emergence of the market model in Eastern Europe, Africa, Latin America, and Asia is no accident. It is not the product of a corporate conspiracy. It is the consequence of hard lessons learned from cold experience. A collectivism that ignores the market will fail. At its worst, it will cost lives. At its best, it will cost prosperity. This is not at all to say that politics is irrelevant, that the market is perfect, that the state is dead, that there are no collective or public purposes to our lives. Quite the contrary: it is that the ingenuity of private individuals is to be prized, that innovation is to be rewarded, that prosperity brings with it real advantages and real improvements in the quality of our lives, and that these lessons should be a premise of sensible public policy.

What is new about globalization ? There has been, after all, international commerce for hundreds of years. From the days of the silk routes, trade has crossed vast continents and oceans and linked the most remote parts of the globe. Certainly the political economists of the nineteenth century, Karl Marx among them, understood that the force of technological change, and the kinds of society required to make that change possible, meant that economic activity and its regulation could no longer be confined to a single country or continent. Consider Marx's description of what was taking place in the middle of the last century, which, rhetoric aside, sounds something like a panegyric from *Forbes* magazine:

> The need of a constantly expanding market for its products chases the bourgeoisie over the whole surface of the globe. It must nestle everywhere, settle everywhere, establish connections everywhere. . . . The bourgeoisie has through its exploitation of the world-market given a cosmopolitan character to production and consumption in every country . . . [and], by the rapid improvement of production, by the immensely facilitated means of communication, draws all, even the most barbarian, nations into civilization. The cheap prices of its commodities are the heavy artillery with which it batters down all Chinese walls, with which it forces the barbarians' intensely obstinate hatred of foreigners to capitulate. It compels all nations, on pain of extinction, to adopt the bourgeois mode of production; it compels them to introduce what it calls civilization into their midst,

i.e. to become bourgeois themselves. In one word, it
creates a world after its own image.[4]

Marx's view was that while the bourgeoisie had
successfully created a global system of capitalism,
their political power would ultimately be obliterated
by an increasingly impoverished working class. Working people around the world would eventually become
masters of this advanced industrial civilization. The
beneficent tutelage of a communist party uniquely
equipped with the necessary values and strategic
intelligence would provide the leadership required to
make this revolution happen.

For a time in the 1960s and 1970s it was an intellectual vogue to suggest that Marx's vision was
essentially a humanistic one, and that it was per-
verted by his followers. There were earnest debates
on the left as to when this perversion had taken
place—before Lenin, after Lenin, by which variety of
faithful.

This debate—which obviously had its parallels in
intense battles in decades before—missed the point
that non-Marxists have understood for generations:
Marx's premises were mainly wrong. His vision was
more than impaired. It was fatally damaged from
the start.

This impairment was both intellectual and moral.
The working classes of the industrialized world were
not fatally impoverished by capitalism. Quite the
opposite: their standard of living rose steadily.

Working people were not increasingly radicalized as they were excluded from the good things of life. They became more conservative as they became more included. The spread of democracy and the universal franchise itself has led to the marginalization not of the people, but of parties which called themselves "Marxist."

Most tragically, the Marxist notion of a party providing the leadership necessary for the dictatorship of the proletariat led only to the dictatorship of the party itself, and then of smaller and smaller cliques within the party, culminating in the cults of Stalin and Mao. This is not some pathetic perversion of Marx, but a perfectly logical consequence of the institutionalized arrogance that was at the heart of his politics.

Apart from a keen sense of economic history, Marx is no guide. Quite the contrary. The dominance of his ways of seeing and interpreting the world has been a disastrous diversion of the twentieth century, which has inflicted untold damage on hundreds of millions of people.

Fortunately the Marxist experiment has been deeply repudiated in virtually every part of the world. In a manner unthinkable a generation ago, there is literally no major society anywhere that embraces the view that collectivist solutions based on the elimination of significant property rights and functioning markets are a better, higher order than some kind of capitalism.

The evolution of social democratic thinking has been more supple on this question, as one would naturally expect. European trade unionists and social activists of the last century would have shared with Marx a deep sense of confidence that history was on their side. They argued that as industry itself was becoming bigger and more collective, the transition to socialism would be gradual and evolutionary, but equally inevitable. By "socialism" there was certainly no division as to what was meant—the ownership and management by the state of the basic means of production and finance. This definition was assumed and widely shared by all parties on the "democratic left" at the end of the nineteenth century, and certainly inspired the earliest pioneers of democratic socialism in Canada and the United States.

The split between democratic and revolutionary socialism was at this point about means rather than ends. Both agreed that private companies above a certain size would be nationalized by the state, and that production would be planned under the wise guidance of experts in a variety of fields. They differed profoundly on the merits of parliamentary democracy. After the Bolshevik Revolution this was not a mere debate. It is often forgotten that after he seized power Lenin's first opponents were those on the left who did not share his intoxication with ruthlessness. They were jailed and killed.

Yet the vision of most democratic socialists was of an economy that would be run from the centre, by the state. It was, essentially, a vision of a national economy in which decisions would be made by a democratically elected government, with the help of scientifically trained experts. Trade would be carried out between states and collectively owned trading corporations, with the best interests of the citizens at heart.

The most important shifts to this kind of thinking began to occur in the 1930s, in response to the impact of real events and real people. Franklin D. Roosevelt showed that governments could improvise, and that capitalism in crisis did not have to lead to chaos and dictatorship. Even Prime Minister R.B. Bennett got the message when he announced his own watered down version of the New Deal, although too late for his own political salvation. The economy became more deliberately mixed, as state enterprise and intervention were used to create work. The Swedish social democratic movement quietly made its peace with the market at the same time, and remained in power for more than forty years. The postwar success of the Marshall Plan in Europe, together with a growing shared realization of the human disaster of the Stalinist experiment, began to influence social democratic thinking as well. The notion of a self-contained, collectively owned, command and control economy had little public appeal and was therefore abandoned as an objective by virtually every democratic socialist party in the world.

In Canada, this debate culminated in the so-called

"Winnipeg Manifesto" of 1956, which was to replace the Regina Manifesto of 1932. For the "eradication of capitalism" promised in the dirty thirties, more modest themes of planning and social security were substituted.

At this point, in the late 1950s, Hugh Gaitskell, who was then Leader of the British Labour Party, forced a debate in his own party on two issues: British commitment to its NATO defence obligations, which meant a rejection of unilateral disarmament, and the need to change the party's constitution, which meant abandoning the commitment to collective ownership and management of the means of production as set out in Clause 4 of the Labour Party's Constitution.

Gaitskell died before he could finish the job of redefining social democracy. Most of his successors preferred to let the ambiguities of a manufactured consensus within the party prevail over the task of creating a very different vision. Harold Wilson, a master of day-to-day survival, once dismissed Gaitskell's efforts as "like telling the Salvation Army there's no salvation."

John Smith, who led the Labour Party for two short years before his premature death in 1994, and Tony Blair, his successor and now British prime minister, realized that they had to complete the task begun a full forty years before by Hugh Gaitskell. Like most changes in life, it was forced on them by the sheer power of external events. But at least they understood that it had to be done.

Margaret Thatcher was elected in 1979, defeating the Labour government of James Callaghan, at least in part because the Labour Party was manifestly unable to persuade the broader trade union movement of the need for discipline and restraint. As the assault led by some unions on the Callaghan government's efforts to achieve a broad social contract grew more vicious and vociferous, the Conservatives were able to present themselves as an alternative with a difference. Margaret Thatcher and her friends and supporters seized the initiative and held on to political power for nearly twenty years.

She stripped trade unions of rights and powers developed over almost a century of steady gains and entitlements. This in turn fostered huge demonstrations and protests, with literally hundreds of thousands on the streets of London and every major city. The counter-revolution continued regardless.

She insisted that Britain become a low-cost producer within Europe. Traditional industries, like steel, coal, textiles, and shipbuilding, were completely decimated, and it took many years for new jobs and work to take their place. When the new work came, it was for less pay, with no union protection. Audiences around the world have laughed long and hard at *The Full Monty*. In addition to being a funny and touching movie, it is a metaphor for Thatcherite Britain. Steelmakers no more, the lads rely on their entrepreneurial ingenuity to become striptease dancers.

Britain's entry into the Common Market, debated with such heat a quarter of a century ago, shattered forever the notion of the sovereign economy. This proved devastating for many on both the left and right of the political spectrum, but ultimately has been accepted by trade unionists, business leaders, and most realists in all parties. It has forced the understanding that the world economy is not "out there," but at home, on the doorstep, and that to suggest that one has to participate, and to compete, in this economy is not a declaration of surrender or capitulation. It is simply a recognition of the way things are.

Tony Blair determined that the Labour Party would only achieve political power if it came to terms at once with its own shortcomings and the changes in the world around it. He insisted that the party literally be "reborn" as the "New Labour Party," that public ownership be abandoned as the end-game of the democratic socialist project, that the permanence of the Thatcherite revolution be simply assumed as a given, and that the world of global capitalism be accepted as the world in which Britain would be living and working.

He decided not to fudge on any of these issues, and to deal with them well before the election of 1996. He staked his leadership on getting the changes made, and made they were. He was thus able to prepare the public and the party for what would come after the election. In contrast to so many elections and so many campaigns, his was not the classic effort of the populist left, in which vast promises were made and easy enemies devastated. The "New Britain" was not

going to be built in that way.

Tony Blair will continue to face the challenge of convincing a great many in his party that the better world they are seeking to build is really better or much different than the one they are living in now. This is really the challenge of all social democratic leaders in the world today, as they have had to come to terms with the dynamism and sheer power of global capitalism. Blair's pragmatism is the clearest public admission that social democracy is now about the improvements we can make to what we have. There will be important debates about who gets what, when, where, and how, and under which prevailing cultural and spiritual values these changes are to be made. But we are not in a transition to a completely different kind of society.

Tony Blair's success, like Franklin Roosevelt's in the 1930s, stands for the proposition that the issue in the modern world is not between capitalism and socialism. It is about what kind of capitalism we want to have. This may seem like a minor point, a definitional quibble. But it is much more than that. It means that a fundamental premise of life for earlier socialists, democratic and revolutionary, that capitalist civilization was so fundamentally corrupt and contradictory that it could not survive, and that it would inevitably be replaced by a completely different way of producing and distributing our worldly goods, is simply wrong.

Writing during the Battle of Britain in 1940, George Orwell was convinced that Britain was in a revolutionary period, and that the war itself was graphic proof that capitalism was grossly inefficient:

> We know very well that with its present social struc-
> ture England cannot survive, and we have got to
> make other people see that fact and act upon it. We
> cannot win the war without introducing socialism,
> nor establish socialism without winning the war.[5]

Three years later he admitted, with refreshing candour, that he had been wrong,

> For after all we have not lost the war, unless appear-
> ances are very deceiving, and we have not introduced
> Socialism. Britain is moving towards a planned econ-
> omy, and class distinctions tend to dwindle, but there
> has been no real shift of power and no increase in
> genuine democracy. The same people still own all the
> property and usurp all the best jobs. In the United
> States the development appears to be away from
> Socialism. The United States is indeed the most pow-
> erful country in the world, and the most capitalistic.[6]

Orwell never lost his assumption that socialism of some kind was better than the capitalist alternative. Neither did other key exponents of social democracy in these years, like R.H. Tawney. In books like *The Acquisitive Society* and *Equality*, Tawney argued for a return to a moral economy that would reflect the desire for a more equal rather than a grasping society. The premise of this economy was, of course, a nation-state which would own and control key industries, and in which all its members would readily accept limits on their wealth.

Tony Blair correctly determined that the Labour Party could never be elected if it stayed locked in the old paradigm. The situation in Canada is less clear. The shift is occurring in those places where the party is either in power or aspires to be in office. Where powerlessness itself is interpreted as a virtue, there is a tendency to revert to nostalgia.

Within Canada, it is still too close to conventional wisdom on the left that globalization is to be feared and opposed. The global economy is a reflection of a "corporate agenda" that is corrupting, because it creates profits for a wealthy elite and only a few crumbs for the people.

Yet the argument that private investment that crosses borders is a bad thing is hardly sustainable. Investment in our own and in other countries is hardly evil. It is not an expression of imperialism. There will be more and more of it in the future. Canadian workers, through their membership in pension funds and their ownership of mutual funds, are significant investors themselves. As provincial and federal rules on foreign investment relax (which, inevitably, they will), it will be in the direct interest of workers to ensure that these investments are treated by other governments with transparency and fair rules.

Investors in Canada can hardly expect less. Surely we don't want governments expropriating property, whoever owns it, without compensation or due process.

Looking at the trade debates in his own country, John Kenneth Galbraith, in his valuable book *The Good Society*, notes the debate on left and right on this issue and then makes this point:

> Few will doubt the force of the basic conflict involved here. How is it resolved in the good society? The solution is not difficult; it has the advantage of inevitability. The move to a closer association between the peoples and institutions of the advanced countries cannot be resisted. It is on the great current of history; the social forces involved are beyond the influence of national legislatures, parliaments and politicians. The oratory may oppose it; the tide still will run. Nor should one wish otherwise. [7]

There was a logic to Prime Minister John A. Macdonald's National Policy more than a hundred years ago. Building up Canadian companies behind the protection of a tariff wall was a reasonable course of action, given the existence of these barriers in so many of our trading partners. Indeed, as late as the

1960s and 1970s it was still possible to speak with coherence of Canada having a national economy.

This is no longer the case for Canada and for a great number of other countries in the world. We are at once too regionalized a country and too integrated into economies and markets beyond our borders for us to usefully talk of "the Canadian economy" as if this were some kind of sovereign entity independent of the world. Yet the pictures in our heads persist, with the resultant desire to cling to policies and nostrums that don't work any more.

Tariffs are gone. Non-tariff barriers to trade and investment are steadily being eliminated. As Galbraith puts it, this is indeed the tide of history. It is pointless devising long statements of policy that attempt to stem the tide. It is far wiser to accept the reality of what is happening and then devise strategies to deal with the consequences. Some of these strategies can only take place at the international level. Yet a great many will remain local and national in scope. Government is neither dead nor irrelevant. It is not a matter of a bigger or smaller public sector. It is a matter of a better, more focused government and public sector, and an understanding that much more will be required at the international level than ever before.

Let me give a couple of examples. Until a few years ago, the Ontario and B.C. grape and wine industries were highly protected. Our farmers produced sweet Concord grapes, which were good for grape juice and sweet wines. The grape juice could, of course, be exported, but it is fair to say that the wine mainly appealed to limited domestic tastes. This industry was subsidized by governments, both federal and provincial, in a number of ways, principally by discriminating against imported wines through higher taxes and much less favourable marketing treatment. Most conventional political opinion subscribed to this arrangement, although an increasingly sophisticated wine-consuming public found the arrangements inconvenient and annoying.

Foreign wine producers found them even more inconvenient and annoying, and took their case to the General Agreement on Tariffs and Trade, the predecessor to the World Trade Organization. GATT eventually ruled against Canada, and discriminatory taxes and prices were no longer allowed.

Governments were at that point left with the choice of doing nothing, which would have meant a not-so-slow death for the farmers and workers in the wine industry, or working out a strategy of adjustment that accepted the inevitability of a world market in wine. We adopted the second approach, and it has worked.

Governments supported the tearing-up of thousands of acres of Concord grapevines and encouraged the cultivation of grape varieties suited both to the region and to the sophisticated wine palate. With the leadership of local wine producers with substantial international experience, we now have a wine industry that can compete successfully on world markets. It also has the strong support of Ontarians, just as the B.C. wine industry has a local base that has allowed it to grow to an international standard.

Globalization is not an evil international conspiracy. Communication and travel bring markets closer together than ever before. People rightly demand the highest standards, the best products. Once these tastes are developed, there is no holding them back. That is what markets and free choices are all about, and why they have won the economic argument.

This does not mean that governments are powerless, or that local loyalties will disappear. In the case of the wine industry, local products sell well because they are good, not because we keep foreign products out or charge a confiscatory tax. Governments intervened to help the industry change: they did not sit back and do nothing.

The same has been true of Canadian cultural policy. It has succeeded more where it has directly encouraged Canadian production and content, not where it has attempted to exclude foreign product. Canadians will not long tolerate being cut off from the global marketplace. They will fully support Canadian producers, but they will also insist on full access to the world.

Turning from a local example to global change, no economic events have been of greater significance in recent years than the "Asian crisis." Just as it is impossible to have a discussion about the local weather without references to El Niño, the prospects for growth in Canada or any country cannot ignore the impact of change in any region of the globe.

The success of the Asian economies since the late 1960s was dramatic. Japan was obviously a special case, its postwar reconstruction leading to a steady boom in the late fifties. Thailand, Taiwan, South Korea, Singapore, Indonesia, and Malaysia had all seen levels of growth for the past twenty years unparalleled anywhere else in the world.

Japan's success stemmed from its earlier commitments to technical education and a strong infrastructure, together with a ruthless determination to protect the home market. Government, business, and financial institutions all worked closely together. Education, rather than health or other social security provisions, was seen as the critical public investment. As costs of production rose in Japan, it invested steadily in lower-wage economies to the south.

The results of this growth were spectacular. The standard of living in each country improved dramatically. They export a full range of products both to each other in the Asian region, and into European and North American markets. According to *The Economist* magazine, 97 per cent of Malaysia's GDP depends on trade. For Taiwan, the figure stands at 70 per cent. Canada is at around 40 per cent, while the U.S. is only at 9.3 per cent (which may help to explain the continuing neo-isolationist vogue in that country).

Yet all economies can get overheated, just as all

economies can enter recessions and even depressions. No country or region has managed to avoid the eventual impact of a business cycle. Equally, all economies rely on debt and credit to function. Financial institutions and banks have to ensure that their loans are matched by their assets, that real security is being provided for loans, and have to provide adequately for higher risk. When this does not happen, the recession in any particular sector, whether mining or real estate, immediately spreads to the financial sector, and from there can have a dramatic effect on the rest of the economy.

A key to the problems in Asia was also one of the original sources of its strength: the strong link between banking, government, and industry. The United States discovered the problem these links can cause at a more local level with the recent savings-and-loan scandal. Local business, political, and financial interests became too chummy, with the resultant bad and shaky loans based on dubious projections of future growth. This is what Whitewater is all about.

This is partly also what South Korea and Thailand's problems are all about, but on a much grander scale. The simple interconnectedness of things (which is really just another way of saying "globalization") means that there are very few local problems any more in the world economy. A serious recession in Asia will not produce an immediate collapse in North America, but it will have a profound effect: it will be harder for us to find ready markets for some of our products and the prices of those products will decline; it will mean Canadian engineering companies will have less work on projects that can no longer be financed; it means that Canadian banks that have been involved in financing exports or investments will have to make more provision for bad loans, and will have to be part of the international efforts to tide over Asian banks that have been caught short. Most important, it means that devalued Asian currencies will boost their exports to Canada, at lower prices, which is good news for consumers but not so good for domestic manufacturing, in particular the auto industry, which will have to further reduce its own costs and prices in order to compete.

Japan's crisis has even greater potential to affect us all. Its banking and manufacturing have been profoundly affected by the collapse in Southeast Asia. Its domestic economy is surprisingly rigid, with many sectors protected from competition. It is impossible to be complacent about the implications of a deep Japanese recession. We are all too interconnected, and Japan's economy is simply too large.

The market-place is more integrated and global than the political institutions that are needed to provide the necessary countervailing balances to private excess. The premise of neo-conservatives is that markets left to their own devices will produce the best possible result, and that political interference is not required. This defies the human reality that people are not commodities, and simply refuse to behave as if they were. This is the story of human history through the ages. The people of Asia, Eastern Europe, and Latin America are no different: they will demand responses from their governments to the human tragedies that are the consequence of bad economic decisions. The difficulty is that local and national governments on their own cannot provide an adequate response.

We do not yet have a politics that is equal to the economics around us. But that is no reason for pessimism, or for a retreat to a narrow nationalism. Nor does it mean that we have to abandon our commitments to people and communities, both our neighbours as well as those in the vast majority around the world who are still very poor. We need strategies at home that recognize that the market-place in which most of us find our work will become even more international and interconnected than ever before, and that certain policies and assumptions about state intervention have to be abandoned. We also need international approaches that affirm our shared commitment to solidarity and values that extend beyond the market-place.

Citizens in industrial countries will be subjected to headlines telling them that their hard-earned tax money is being siphoned off to support bankers in far-off countries, and their immediate response will be gloomy. Yet if the alternative is a virtual collapse of the economies of Mexico, South Korea, or Thailand, it is hard to see the logic or wisdom of letting these things happen when we know they can be avoided.

Think Roosevelt on a global scale. "Bail-outs" are always seen as a bad thing when they're being done for someone else, yet surely that is exactly what self-interest would dictate if drowning is the only alter-native. When large companies and banks drown, they tend to pull a lot of us down with them. Which is a good reason to think of ways to avoid such calamities, either locally or far away.

The connection between Ontario wine and Asian banks is that neither protectionism nor complete *laissez-faire* is really the answer. In the one case, a local solution had to be found that would ensure some chance of economic success in a different and expanded market-place. In the other, domestic solu-tions are inadequate, and broader intervention is required. In both cases, better answers will be found if there is a continuing commitment to using public policy, both locally and internationally, to finding solutions, and in rejecting the twin excesses of throwing up walls and throwing up our hands.

The turmoil in world markets is ample proof that no country is an island. Russia's collapse is a calamity for her prople. The privatization process so enthusi-astically forced by international institutions has given a corrupt advantage to a small minority. Criminal capitalism has seized control. A weakened state and civil society cannot respond.

But those banks and others who have invested in Russia are caught in the collapse as well. Previously-healthy institutions may be undermined.

In fact the world economy is now facing a challenge of overcapacity, too many short term national decisions, international solutions long on ideology, and an absence of leadershp. We need a new Marshall Plan, but not just for one country. We need to build local demand instead of forcing every new economy to starve the real economy and produce more exports. We need lower interest rates in the U.S., Europe, and Japan. We need to focus investment on the enormous requirements of a healthy infrastructure.

Trade unions have been key elements of the social democratic movement since the industrial revolution. The challenges faced today pose dramatic choices. Hillel's three questions put these choices in an interesting perspective.

The very existence of trade unions is an answer to the first question: the industrial and bureaucratic workplace gave rise to a sense of collective self-interest. The solidarity of feeling among men and women facing a common employer was eventually supported by a public policy that required greater balance. Management power could not be exclusive.

There is a growing awareness that this expression of self-interest, as essential as it is for the protection of wages and living standards, is still not enough. Unions have long participated in broader social and political movements. They have also sought to broaden their membership across trades, skills, and national boundaries.

This move to change and merge will undoubtedly

continue. The need for more effective international groupings of labour to match both the reach of transnational companies and the emergence of stronger intergovernmental agreements will grow. Purely national labour institutions will find it more difficult to do their job. The career of the eighteenth-century democratic pioneer Thomas Paine spanned three countries and two revolutions: he felt in his bones that the spirit of popular feeling transcended borders and cultures. He would have understood immediately the phrase about the American Revolution: "the shot heard round the world." The technology of television and now the Internet means that no slum, no unhealthy factory, no dictatorship can avoid the antiseptic spotlight of public attention. Globalization is not just for business.

Consumer boycotts will be an increasing weapon of trade unions and other organizations whose capacity for research and education extends beyond the doors of the local unions. If well organized and coordinated to touch a responsive chord in public opinion, they will succeed.

Hillel's second question points to a second change already well underway. The unions' classic demand for "more" cannot be made with a wilful ignorance of the economics of the enterprise, whether private, nonprofit, or governmental. In some cases, unions have even been forced by the drastic changes in the economy to assume ownership of the company itself. Some have resisted and opposed these changes with the traditional accusation that the workers' interests have been "sold out." But this misses the point that saving companies and jobs is just as much a worker's respon-

sibility as anyone else's, and perhaps even more in their interest.

In point of fact, these decisions are made all the time as labour disputes are avoided or settled. Labour and management are forced to answer Hillel's question when they realize they can't be just for themselves. And the speed and force of change and the existence of hungry competitors forces the answer to the third question.

———◆———

The End of Government?

IN HER RECENT BOOK *The Retreat of the State*, SUSAN Strange has convincingly written about technological change occurring at a pace unimaginable to previous generations:

> No one under the age of thirty or thirty-five today needs convincing that, just in their lifetime, the pace of technological change has been getting faster and faster. The technically unsophisticated worlds of business, government and education of even the 1960s would be unrecognisable to them. No fax, personal computers, no accessible copiers, no mobile phones, no video shops, no DNA tests, no cable TV, no satellite networks connecting distant markets twenty-four hours a day. The world in which their grandparents grew

up in the 1930s or 1940s is as alien to them as that
of the Middle Ages. . . .

This simple, everyday, common sense fact of modern life is important because it goes a long way to
explaining both political and economic change. It
illuminates the changes both in the power of states
and in the power of markets. Its dynamism, in fact,
is basic to my argument, because it is a continuing
factor, not a once-for-all change.[1]

The pace of these changes and the fact that many
of them lie outside the control of politics and governments is critical to understanding how the world
around us is being transformed. Harold Innis, one
of Canada's great historians and thinkers, based
his work in economic history on the notion that
understanding the technological basis of a society's
economy would help to explain the broader social
and political framework. Understand the staple at
the heart of the economy, and this would explain
much else.

The Canada of cod and fur is infinitely more marginal than ever before. The Canada of the railways
and timber still exists, but is far less dominant. The
Canada of the digital economy, which will become
increasingly more important as time unfolds, will
inevitably be more decentralized, flexible, and open
than what was there before. The central state will
have less power as transnational corporations assume
greater dominance in each sector of the economy, as

transborder flows of capital increase at a bewildering
pace each day, and as decisions taken at a trader's desk
in any financial capital have immediate consequences
for the most distant society.

We are thus faced with the paradox that our economic world has become at once more local and more
global. This is because the technologies that are at the
heart of the information economy are decentralizing,
while the companies that are the key carriers of the
technology are increasingly global in their reach.
Some decry these changes, and attempt valiantly to
resist them. They will not succeed. As Susan Strange
puts it bluntly:

> This shift, already under way but by no means
> finished, is a consequence not of state authority but
> of the power of markets and of corporate strategies
> responding to markets. It is already causing eco-
> nomic pain, in America, in Europe and not least in
> Japan; and there is often strong political opposition
> to any kind of liberalisation of trade or immigra-
> tion rules that is thought to make the pain worse.
> Again, history is a good guide. This is not the first
> time that economic change has brought a redistri-
> bution of income in society. And on other occa-
> sions—with the shift from wealth and employment
> derived from manufacturing—there was political
> protest and fierce resistance. That can be expected
> again. But as before, the Luddites, the Chartists and
> all the other losers from change and redistribution

will not succeed in reversing the trend. State policies may help to assuage or slow down the adjustment. They will not stop the need for it. And the
economic system, as before, will probably benefit.
More new producers of wealth means more new
consumers. The additional demand will stimulate
further investment and more employment, though
not always in the same places or for the same people
as in the past.[2]

Think of the general array of economic solutions
popular among interventionists in the past and, even
the present: tariff barriers, strategies of import sub-
stitution, purchasing power solutions to create
domestic industries (think of the "Ontario computer
for education" in brief vogue in the 1970s and 1980s),
designated "national products" to replace imports
(like "national cars"), non-tariff barriers designed to
increase local production and force companies to do
business locally in exchange for access to domestic
markets. These will all dwindle, although there will
always be those urging their use and application,
even if world trade obligations make them unen-
forceable and even unlawful. Larger countries, like
the U.S. and China, will have greater success in
imposing them (like the "Buy America" laws passed
by the U.S. Congress which require mass-transit
manufacturers to establish facilities in the United
States if they want to sell to the U.S. cities receiv-
ing a federal subsidy for their subways). Smaller

countries like Canada will find it harder to impose similar patterns.

The picture in our heads of trade is still of an activity taking place between sovereign countries. This is misleading. Trade happens within companies and between companies. Governments can encourage it, and promote it. If they own Crown corporations, they of course do it themselves, but they do this in their role as market actors. Trade missions like "Team Canada" can help to make a case before other governments that Canadian companies should be given fair access to local markets, but it is a stretch for governments to claim that they make the deals happen, and an illusion to think of the trade as between "Canada" and "China." It will more and more be between companies in Canada and companies in China.

What, then, is left of sovereignty and the state ? Is politics made irrelevant by the triumph of technology and the market ? Is this all just an argument for business and the "corporate agenda"?

Francis Fukuyama, the American social scientist, has written two books on this very subject, *The End of History* and *Trust.*[3] In the first he argues that while Marx's view that history would "end" with the transition to communism became a destructive illusion, there is merit in an historical approach to human and technological evolution. Liberal democracy, in his view, is about as good as it gets, and it is difficult even to imagine a society which, given our knowledge of alternatives and human nature, would be better. In this sense, he argues, liberal democracy represents the end of history. There is nothing better to which we can realistically and morally aspire, and there is reason to believe that, allowing for some terrible steps backwards and sideways, other societies will eventually evolve to this condition as well. The appeal of free markets and new technologies, together with the rising standards of living with which they are associated, will become irresistible to all people and all cultures. The difference with Marx is that there is no reason to aspire further to socialism or communism. These have been tried and have failed. They may be tried again, writes Fukuyama, but they will not succeed, because they are too fundamentally flawed.

In his next book, *Trust*, Fukuyama points out that liberal democratic capitalism can take a variety of forms in a number of different cultures, and that civil societies depend as much on a high level of trust as on a body of law. By civil societies, Fukuyama means those based on a respect for the rights of the individual, including the rights of property. They recognize that open markets, effectively scrutinized, have proven to be the most efficient way to provide for the economic needs of people. Countries where governments intrude too far into the economy, by owning too much and by seeking to regulate too much, fall behind economically. Yet the market cannot, and should not, do everything. Civil societies, therefore, value the role of government and understand that the size of the public sector will naturally depend on shifting public needs and demands. In this context, civil societies depend on bureaucracies that are free of corruption, are open, and are noted for their professional efficiency.

Civil societies are plural societies in the sense that there are many centres of power and authority, not just one. Corporations, both for-profit and non-profit, have an independent role and are respected as such. Institutions of higher learning are free of political interference, and education and the growth of knowledge are seen as good things in themselves. Voluntary associations of all kinds are encouraged, as are trade unions and other organizations whose purpose is the improvement of the condition of the people.

Civil societies are based on the premise that an independent judiciary and a legal system with a transparent ability to maintain order and protect rights are essential. Civil societies must include a free press that is subject to laws of libel, but is free from political repression or censorship. We know that a free and independent press is vital to the functioning of economic as well as political markets. Civil societies, as their name implies, are based on a respect for public order, as well as a civility of discourse. In this sense, civil societies are based on a high level of social trust and mutual confidence.

Fukuyama is right that the collapse of the Berlin

Wall ended 140 years of the Marxist illusion. But there has been a profound debate about how capitalism can evolve, and the politics that this requires, quite outside the Marxist paradigm. History has only ended for those caught inside the Marxist hothouse. For the rest of us the argument is just getting interesting.

People may work in the market, and we certainly buy in it as consumers. But this is hardly the sum total of our existence. We live in families, and we define an important part of our lives as children, parents, husbands, wives, lovers, and friends. We also live in communities and countries where we think of ourselves as citizens. It is absurd to deny the validity or worth of any of these senses of who we are. It is perverse to ask that we pursue one or other exclusively at the expense of all others. They are all important. Each also informs the other. No sphere is entirely self-contained or exclusive. Our sense of who we are as parents informs our views about politics, just as does the role we play in the economy.

We are recovering from a century where politics has promised too much. It would be an equal mistake to enter the next with the public sphere offering too little. The economy and the corporate agenda are not the only things that are global. So are our sense of human rights and dignity. So is the environment. They deserve an equal claim. They do not have it yet, and building the necessary democratic countervails to the global reach of the economy will take much effort.

Hillel's first question, then, points to the permanence of self-interest: but that self-interest can take many forms. It can be the self-interest of the company in the market. It can speak to the collective self-interest of the trade unionist or country faced with the power of international institutions. The globalized, high technology world is the product of the culture of self-interest, and in turn fuels the politics and economics of self-interest in every part of the world.

It is fashionable in some quarters to speak of the end of government, of its complete irrelevance in the face of these global forces. This simplistic view ignores some basic facts. First, government and the public sector remain huge facts in our lives. Second, globalization is not just a corporate event. Bill Clinton can go to China and engage in a debate about human rights precisely because China is not isolated. The economic exchanges of the last twenty years have not just changed the Chinese economy. They have created a very different human dynamic that no leadership can ignore.

The clear thrust of the decisions taken in China, for example, is that the relationship between the market and the state is going to be tipped farther in favour of the market, but the state will need to be reformed and strengthened as well. The central lesson of European social democracy of the fifties and sixties—that the state does not need to, and indeed in the interest of efficiency should not, own goods-and-services producing industries—is about to be applied in China on a wider scale than ever before.

The momentousness of this decision is made greater because the state-owned enterprises have played the dominant role in delivering social services to their employees. The Chinese public sector will be reducing its role as an owner and producer. At the same time, it will have to strengthen its role as a provider of the social safety net. In other words, industry will be increasingly privatized and other services will be more comprehensively socialized. Thus China will evolve toward a modern welfare state.

This transition will, of course, be an enormous challenge. A great many of the state-owned enterprises in the old closed economy have been losing money, and have depended on state banks to fund their losses. The transition to competitive enterprise will be painful, and China will experience high levels of unemployment and under-employment that have previously been masked by the old regime.

These are not philosophical or ideological issues. They are matters of practical judgement. The institutions of the public sector—effective regulation, efficient public services, dramatic improvements in education, training, health care and social security, strong markets, and the enhancement of the rule of law—are just as important as creating modern companies capable of competing internationally without the benefit of subsidies. It is not a matter of more or less government. It is a question of the institutions of government and civil society refocusing. Strong markets require an effective state.

Countries that have benefited greatly from foreign investment—and that includes every major Asian economy, including China—have to accept the logic of greater openness, transparency, better regulation, and a better mix of public and private policy. At the same time, the institutions of the world economy have to be as strongly committed to stability as Franklin Roosevelt was in the age of the national economy. This is the true logic of globalization: an international willingness to prevent excess and temporary crisis from becoming a disaster. This collective will and sense of calm and confidence require leadership.

The strengthening of all the institutions of civil society and the appreciation of the importance of good governance of modern economies will contribute to the expansion of human and civil rights. Citizenship, with all its rights and responsibilities, will become as important as consumerism. There are signs of that everywhere—and nowhere more strongly than in Hong Kong. The rule of law, the respect for family and the individual, the commitment to education: these are all key values in the development of civil societies everywhere. In Hong Kong they have been accompanied by a growing commitment to democracy as well. It is hard to see how the advantages of freedom and civil order will not spread to China itself, recognizing at the same time the preoccupation of the leadership with the question of stability. There is an irresistible logic to democracy which cannot be ignored.

The debates about governance and its importance cannot be confined to developing economies. Governmental bureaucracies are being forced to change in every part of the world. It is hard to see why corporate structures should not change as well. Corporate boards are, for the most part, unreflective of the broader public and have difficulty responding to the power of an entrenched management.

Employees themselves are rarely represented as legitimate stakeholders within the company's corporate structure, partly because many unions prefer the comfortable pew of permanent opposition, but mainly because management is more comfortable with relatively safe appointees from the same club.

This attitude will have to change, partly because the shareholding structure of a more democratic economy should no longer permit such hidebound exclusiveness. Company presidents with huge salaries and stock options who dine only in their own chosen company at the top of some vast tower are not an inevitable feature of a market economy. They are an outmoded expression of privilege. A less deferential,

more open, and more democratic economy is not
synonymous with radicalism, let alone socialism.
Even monarchies have different styles—the corporate
world can reform itself if it chooses. If it does not, the   · 59 ·
pressure for change and accountability can only grow.

Self-Interest and the Public Interest: Taxes, Debts, and Deficits

AS EVEN *The Economist,* THAT CLARION VOICE OF
nineteenth-century political economy, has pointed
out, the state and politics are hardly dead.[1] The public sector accounts for anywhere between 30 and 50
per cent of economic activity in the industrialized
countries of the world, which can hardly be called
insignificant. Even after nearly twenty years of the
Reagan-Thatcher ascendancy, tax-takes of more than
40 per cent are common in most countries. There has
certainly been a rhetorical shift in many countries
towards the market, and away from politics. But, like
Mark Twain's, reports of the death of the public sector and of politics are greatly exaggerated.

Governments remain responsible for setting policy,
and in most cases for providing the necessary services,

for law and order, defence, health care, education and training, welfare, help to the disabled, social housing, pensions and support for the elderly, cultural institutions, and a myriad of other policy areas from trade and international human rights to environmental policy and natural resource management. To suggest that in the global market-place of the twenty-first century there will be no role for the state and the public sector is clearly nonsense.

What is at issue is the national economy's and public's willingness and ability to pay for the cost of continuing to provide these services in an age of diminishing borders. At times this has been presented as a simple issue of "making the rich pay." Statistics are trotted out showing that corporations paid a lot more tax in the 1940s and 1950s, and pay less now, and that if we could only put the burden back up on rich people and corporations the problem would be solved "hey presto."

Would that life were that easy. There are two issues to consider here. One is globalization itself, the end of capital controls, and the fact that virtually all industrial economies are more or less open. The second is the end of inflation. Both combine to create the phenomenon of what has been described as "the disappearing taxpayer."[2] When "American" corporations earn 50 per cent or more of their earnings outside the country, a pattern that can be matched by any transnational companies, the question of comparative corporate tax rates can be a crucial factor in retaining and attracting new investment. Companies will gauge their profits and pricing according to the most beneficial tax effect, which is hardly surprising.

The shift to the personal income tax becomes · 65 · equally problematic. Local tax rates for individuals become a significant factor for executive and managerial recruitment. Equally, as self-employment increases and the number of full-time employees declines, it becomes easier for individuals to avoid some taxation. Consultants with allowable expenses pay less tax than employees with very few such benefits.

This is all before the expansion of activities on the Internet, which will involve an area of commerce that is exceedingly hard to tax. One approach suggested is an international tax on financial transactions, the so-called "Tobin tax," which is attractive theoretically, but hard to administer. It would be readily avoided by creating tax-free havens that would naturally expand as the focus for financial activity. This is another example where the absence of coherent international governance makes such tax regimes difficult in practice, however desirable in the best of all possible worlds. After all, it is really just an extension of the VAT principle to another level of transaction and service that is transborder in scope.

Taxes on wealth and corporate activity have to take into account of the increased mobility of capital. This means that there will continue to be pressure on the ordinary middle- and low-income person, particularly since the demand for decent public services will hardly decline, and even with decreasing deficits there is still a 15 to 30 per cent annual tribute that must be paid to the public debt.

If capital flight is one issue for tax policy, low inflation is certainly another. Inflation has always allowed tax increases to be concealed in the apparently never-ending spiral of higher prices and higher incomes. Higher consumption taxes, like a gasoline tax, for example, were less visible when prices were increasing steadily anyway. Higher income taxes could be concealed by a nominal pay increase on the first of January of any year. It is no coincidence that the period of the greatest increase in the size of the public sector and of the public debt in recent times coincided with a period of high inflation. This is not necessarily to argue economic cause and effect. My point is different. Higher taxes were politically possible because their impact on the public was concealed, or at least buffered, by inflation.

It is equally no accident that the period of sustained tax fatigue in a number of countries has coincided with a dramatic reduction in inflation. In a time of flat prices, and flat and even declining incomes, a tax increase of any kind is impossible to conceal. The pay cheque on January 15 is lower than the one on December 31. Speaking from brutal experience, politicians who can't figure this out, or who appeal to a general sense of generosity in the population, will be appropriately thanked and then dismissed by the electorate. Some social democrats like Tony Blair and

Roy Romanow have understood this. Those that haven't are either in opposition or writing books.

The conservative writer and contemporary historian Lord Robert Skidelsky has written in *After Communism* that governments should be reducing their tax take to no more than 30 per cent of the GDP of any economy. That would be a dramatic reduction from where we are today. In Canada it would require a further reduction in public expenditure of about a quarter, which is substantial by any stretch. There can be no doubt that the right will continue to define itself by its commitment to lower taxes, and may indeed set targets as ambitious as those of Lord Skidelsky. One might well ask why not 20 or 25 per cent as the golden target?[3]

A numerical target such as that suggested by the good lord is just a gimmick unless combined with a clear way of getting there. Everyone has to understand the implications of a dramatic reduction in taxes: public services will inevitably become less public. No country can long afford what might be called a European level of social and health service and an American level of taxes. Indeed, one way of looking at the thirty years post 1967 is to see them as the time in which we systematically borrowed more than we were taking in, in order to sustain a standard of living and growth to which we had become accustomed, and to which we believed we were entitled.

The neo-conservative strategy set out by Ronald Reagan after 1980 was to cut taxes and increase defence spending, and then slowly and steadily wait for the pressure to build on the rest of the public sector as the deficit ballooned to unprecedented levels.

The apostle of good cheer, he left the mop-up work to George Bush and Bill Clinton. The truth is that if American taxes on gasoline, liquor, and cigarettes had matched Canada's, the U.S. would not have had a deficit problem. If they had matched the Europeans, the story would have been even more dramatic.

The right has now gone further and suggested for some time that national governments should be prevented by law from running deficits at all. This would mean that while ordinary citizens could continue to borrow money to buy a house or a car, and companies could borrow money to make investments, the public sector would be prevented from similar access to debt as a method of financing any expenditures. Let me quote Galbraith again:

> There are times in modern history and experience when the enunciation of even the most elementary common sense has an aspect of eccentricity, irrationality, even mild insanity. Such is the risk that is run by anyone in the United States who challenges the current commitment to reducing and eliminating the government deficit, this being the overall excess of expenditure over income in the current accounts.[4]

To establish a legal requirement that the budget of a government be completely balanced in every given year is a bad idea. This is not to say that deficit and debt are unimportant or irrelevant; only that they have to be analyzed in a practical manner. No company or individual would accept the notion that, by law, their expenditure has to be matched by income in every year. This would prevent almost everyone, certainly everyone except the very rich, from doing the things many people associate with ordinary life, like buying a house and a car. It would stop almost every company from making any investments.

The test for public indebtedness should be very similar to the one we apply to our own affairs, and which company directors apply to management's request for approval for bonds and debentures as a method of financing an acquisition or any other investment. Is money being borrowed for a long-term purpose of investment, and does the public purse have the means to finance the debt without crowding out spending on necessary current needs? We all know from our visits to the bank manager that this is what she wants to know. A mortgage is not evil, nor is it a sign of profligacy. We only get into trouble when we've borrowed too much, and when our cash flow can't meet the payments. That's when we get into the spiral of borrowing from MasterCard to pay our Visa, and increasing the mortgage to finance a holiday or pay for our children's braces.

Most states in the United States have a legal requirement to balance the budget every year, but they are permitted to make capital expenditures with bonds set aside for this purpose. In some jurisdictions they have to seek a special approval by way of referendum for such long-term bonds. American municipalities work in the same financial context, with stricter external controls on their ability to tap the bond markets, but with the additional advantage that these municipal bonds are tax deductible.

In Canada our public finances have been less clear about the distinction between current expenses and longer-term investments. This is at least in part because these distinctions are not easily made. We commonly speak of education as an investment. Does this include all education expenditure, or just part of it? The Canadian Institute of Chartered Accountants, hardly a revolutionary body, has recently published new guidelines for governments on what they call "tangible capital assets," which include such things as roads, buildings, and vehicles, but do not apply to "intangibles" like natural resources and Crown lands which have not been purchased by government. This is still a step in the right direction, since it will force governments to prepare a better inventory of public assets, to account for them, and to get some appreciation of the fact that a good part of the mortgage or public debt we have built up over the years has been used to improve the quality of life or the common good.

For several years now we have been hearing the incantation that we can't leave a debt to our children. When one analyzes the phrase, we realize how rhetorical and exaggerated it is. It is not unreasonable, on the face of it, to leave our children with an affordable public mortgage, provided it meets the tests set out earlier. If a portion of their taxes is spent · 71 · to finance the debt, there is nothing wrong and everything right with that, assuming, of course, that in addition to the mortgage we have left them schools, teachers, hospitals, doctors, nurses, roads, subways, museums, forests, parks, libraries, and a sense that we owe each other something. Equally important, however, is to face up to why we have had a problem with debts and deficits in Canada.

It was a premise of Keynesian economics that governments should be cutting interest rates and taxes and raising public expenditure when the economy was less than fully employed—in other words, when people were "saving too much" with the resultant unemployment and idle resources. This was the basis of the Kennedy tax cut in 1962, and was more widely applied in the 1970s, resulting in Richard Nixon's famous remark "we're all Keynesians now." Keynes's approach was rejected by the Labour government in Britain after 1929 as too radical. Roosevelt met Keynes, and had many advisers who considered themselves followers, but it would be hard to ascribe the incredible twists and turns of his policy to any particular theory. The world was still in deep recession at the beginning of World War II.

It was war itself which put Keynes to the test. Governments of all countries borrowed massively to meet the cost of fighting Hitler, and increased taxes as well. What is interesting is to note what virtually all Western countries did after the war: they ran surpluses to begin paying down the debt and reducing the burden on the fisc. They did this in concert, and they did it by maintaining tax levels for both individuals and corporations. The strongest sustained economic growth in the century did the rest.

We have to look at the postwar period from a financial point of view in three parts: the period 1945–1970, which was a time of low inflation, low unemployment, and sound public finances; the period from 1970 to about 1992, which was characterized by slow growth (three major recessions), high inflation, high unemployment, and large public-sector deficits; and the period from 1992 on, which has seen slightly improved growth, low inflation, persistent unemployment, and reduced public spending and deficits.

Globalization has played its part here as well. Writing fifty years ago, Keynes certainly understood the impact that international decisions could have on domestic policy. Indeed his greatest polemical tract, *The Economic Consequences of the Peace*, written c. 1920, was an argument that extracting too much out of Germany would end up causing problems everywhere, which turned out to be true. He was also an architect of the postwar reconstruction of international finance at Bretton Woods. But despite this, the key fact for Keynes's policies was the existence of significant tariff barriers in each industrial country.

His assumption was that the stimulus he wanted could be managed within the boundaries of the nation-state.

This is definitely not as true today, and is certainly less true of smaller, trade-based economies than larger, more self-sufficient economies. Canada can stimulate demand by lowering interest rates, cutting taxes, and raising spending, but this may have only a marginal impact on jobs and employment. Many jobs in manufacturing depend not so much on Canadian demand as on international conditions. We're just not as self-enclosed and sovereign as our public rhetoric would like us to believe.

France learned this lesson the hard way in 1980, just as Ontario did after 1991. If everyone else is cutting back, the local attempt to stimulate will simply not be effective. There have to be broader, common strategies. They will not succeed at the level of the nation-state alone, let alone the region. This is not to say that Keynes's insights are now without value; only that they have to be applied with judgement and intelligence.

The near-quarter century of stagflation from 1970 to 1992 came with a price. General levels of indebtedness increased throughout society. This was a personal phenomenon as much as a corporate or political one. The baby boom generation, looking back with confidence at how far their parents had come, wanted the good things in life more quickly, and were prepared to go into debt to get them. Companies have borrowed at unprecedented levels, assuming future cash flows would justify the leverage. Sometimes they have been proven right, sometimes wrong, with occasionally destructive effects.

Conservative commentators often refer to the debts and deficits of the public sector as if they fall from the skies, as if they can somehow be separated from the habits and desires of the public, or from what is happening in the rest of the economy. Deficits rose too quickly in a number of countries and regions from the mid-1970s on, but for reasons that are entirely understandable. In the U.S. the trend was related to the determined strategy of the Reaganites. In Canada it began with a desire to deal with the impact of the three recessions, one in each decade.

Governments then discovered the simple truth that it is easier to get into debt than to get out of it. Periods of growth were marked by a reduction in deficits but never a reduction in the mortgage itself. The result was that each recession left an even bigger mortgage, just as it left an even larger number of unemployed. It was possible to continue the pattern as long as inflation enabled governments to raise taxes, and thus finance the debt. This mould was broken when inflation ended in the early 1990s.

At that point most governments in Canada, of a variety of stripes, concluded that the party couldn't continue. Some did so with ideological enthusiasm; others with greater reluctance. But the broad consensus to change course was well established by 1992.

The conclusion of the postwar boom brought with it the most progressive period in Canadian government in generations, the Pearson welfare state reforms of the mid-1960s. A generation educated in the 1930s and 1940s, armed with the experience of the Depression and World War II, as well as the return to managed prosperity in the 1950s, confidently turned its attention to the need to complete the basic elements of a welfare state: support for those in need, health care, training, and pensions. There was no doubt in the minds of this generation that the leadership for these reforms would come from the federal government in Ottawa, no doubt that it could be paid for, and no doubt that once they saw the transfer money involved, the provinces would fall into line.

The resultant legislation, the Canada Assistance Plan, the Canada Pension Plan, and the laws establishing universal health insurance in all the provinces and territories, established the principle that the federal government would set national standards for welfare, health care, and pensions, and in turn would provide the provinces with an assured 50 per cent of the cost of the programmes, which would in turn be governed by provincial legislation.

The Canada Pension Plan came into existence only after the federal government agreed to let Quebec opt out of the plan and establish its own, parallel plan with similar rules for vesting and portability compatible with the principle that people would move around and needed to be able to maintain a consistent level of contribution and benefit. As a result, Quebec was able to create a fund, the Caisse de Dépôt, that has been a key ingredient in the industrial and economic

transformation of Quebec society. No other province has sought to opt out of the national plan, although there are provisions that would allow for just such an eventuality.

At the end of the 1970s, after the post-oil-crisis slowdown, the federal government decided that the 50 per cent deal was off. It was to be replaced by block transfers of money, as well as the transfer of certain tax points. The writing was on the wall. The federal government had created federal-provincial programmes under a generous umbrella born of the confidence of another time, and the provinces had bought into full participation in the programmes on the basis of the original partnership. The terms of the partnership were being changed, unilaterally, by the federal government. From budget to budget the federal government would announce new reductions in transfers, always unilaterally. The Mulroney government announced that the three "wealthy" provinces of Alberta, British Columbia, and Ontario would be capped in their transfers for provincial welfare. This came right at the beginning of the 1990 recession in Ontario, with serious financial consequences. A court challenge brought the judgement from the Supreme Court of Canada that since the original legislation was an act of the federal parliament, the federal government could act unilaterally if it chose to do so.

The Chrétien government went one better, repealing the Canada Assistance Act altogether. The result is that the range of programmes associated with the welfare state, namely welfare itself, help for the disabled and distressed, and health care of all kinds, are increasingly the sole financial responsibility of the provinces. The federal government likes to wave its flag and insist on its role, but it is no longer a serious and reliable financial partner. The signs of deterioration are everywhere, and date back a full generation.

The federal government has achieved its improved financial situation by cutting hard and deep at the basic fabric of the welfare state. In so doing it has become less of a national government. The regions and provinces have grown in importance by force of circumstance. The principle of "he who pays the piper calls the tune" clearly applies. "National standards" can only be the result of a strong financial presence. As this diminishes, the standards will increasingly be set at local levels.

The economic logic of devolution does not stop there. At the provincial level, the depth of the federal cuts could only be met by increased borrowing for so long, particularly when combined with the reduced revenues of a deep recession. The Harris Tories have run hard with the Big Lie that Ontario was facing bankruptcy after the "ten lost years" of profligate waste by Liberals and the NDP. Like Reagan before him, Harris benefits from a pliant business press and propaganda machine, as well as from an economy that has been growing. But the Tories have been misleading the public systematically about public finances and the choices they have faced since 1995. They needed to create the illusion of a crisis to justify the authoritarian nature of their solutions. There is confusion about what they have devolved and what has been recentralized.

Welfare payments were cut by more than 20 per cent, which meant that the incomes of the most vulnerable were cut more drastically and more quickly than any other "transfer agency." The municipalities will continue to foot part of the welfare bill. Social housing has been forced down to the local level, which means that neither the federal nor the provincial government is involved in affordable housing. This is precisely where we were during the Depression, when the Bruce Report on housing was commissioned in 1934 by the Ontario provincial government of the day. It established beyond any reasonable doubt that the market, left to itself, would never deal with the housing problems of poorer people. This has been borne out by the experience of every modern industrial country. Local governments do not, at this point, have the means to address the problem, which means it will get worse.

Educational policy has been completely centralized. That is what the teachers' dispute was all about. Bargaining between teachers and school boards will continue to be local, but will not deal with the pension issue, which is provincial. School boards and property taxpayers will continue to pay for about 40 per cent of school budgets, which will no doubt add to the confusion.

The principle of devolution, what the Europeans call "subsidiarity" can be a good one, if it is matched by a transfer of resources, and if provincial and federal governments use tax policy wisely. The advantage of downloading is that municipal governments become accountable for spending money and providing services. For certain services, like transportation, municipal governments must have the means to pay for the service over and above what is collected at the fare box. If they impose new taxes, or tolls, or fees, these are not done on a progressive basis, but with cost recovery in mind. That in turn means that there is even more reason for governments with responsibility for income tax to make it even more progressive, i.e. to ensure a larger break for lower- and middle-income people, rather than the biggest breaks for people at the top. This is not being done at the moment. The largest tax breaks will go to those who are best off. This means that the way downloading is being done further increases the trend to inequality, and ensures that the most vulnerable and marginal people will become even more so.

The cost of the Harris tax cut for its first two years was $5.6 billion. Now it is running at about $5 billion per year. Fifty per cent of tax filers earn less than $33,000 per year, and they will receive on average about $350 each. Tax filers earning more than $250,000 will receive more than $15,000 each. To describe this as perverse is inadequate. It becomes even stranger when one calculates that in an economy that will have had good growth for five years, the Harris government will have increased the provincial debt by about $30 billion on the expiry of its first term.

It is interesting to note that in a recent publication, *The Ontario Alternative Budget Papers*, a coalition of social activists brought together by the Ontario Federation of Labour had this to say about debts and deficits:

> Debt levels that are this high, relative to the size of the provincial economy, are clearly not sustainable. A growing debt-to-GDP requires that an increasing proportion of the provincial budget be devoted to public debt interest payments. When interest rates exceed the rate of economic growth, as they have for most of the past ten years, the problem becomes even worse. At $8.7 billion, Ontario's public debt interest payment is the province's third largest budget item. Budgets need to be in balance on average over the business cycle to prevent the public sector from becoming totally mortgaged to banks and international money-lenders. These institutions are the principal beneficiaries of Ontario's huge annual interest payments. The increasing share of the provincial budget that goes to interest payments causes a

number of serious problems. It makes it harder to
pay for public programs. It forces taxes up even when
program spending is not increasing. It reduces the
flexibility of the government to fund new social and
economic programs in times of recession or disloca-
tion. It transfers wealth from taxpayers to money-
lenders.[5]

I couldn't have put it better myself, although I did
try, in a number of speeches after 1992. It is gratify-
ing that six years later the arguments are now generally accepted.

The exposure of every level of government to the
penetrating tests of the international market-place
will not diminish. Canadian governments tried hard
after 1975 (like many others) to buy time and protection. The federal government began borrowing,
taxing, and off-loading; so, in turn, did the provinces
and many local governments. The buck has finally
stopped.

The first reaction is for people to look for someone
to blame, and to push political hot-buttons. We lash
out at governments, politicians. In ugly moods we lash
out at immigrants and people on social assistance.

Canadians are subject to these moods like all others. We compound it with particular regional resentments. Canadians were surprised when even Ontario
joined the ranks of the regionally aggrieved. No one
should be surprised. Treat us like a region, as began
to happen most emphatically after 1975, and that is

how we shall respond. This political fact has been bottled up by the vast Liberal majority in Ontario since 1993, but it will inevitably re-emerge.

· 82 ·   The challenge is to find the institutional ways across the country of ensuring that some limits are placed on exaggerated regional or sectional feeling. In the case of Quebec, this has always been unusually difficult, since we are dealing here not with local grievance alone but with a persistent ethnic nationalism which since the 1960s has insisted on the break-up of the country as a prelude to an undefined "association" or "partnership."

This nationalism is in turn fuelled by a myth that there is a single English-speaking Canada—against which it is fashionable in Quebec to rail and complain. What regionalism in the midst of globalization really means is that there is no "there" there: English-speaking Canada exists much less clearly than it did even twenty or thirty years ago. Canada, contrary to the mythology of Mr. Bouchard, is not some external force apart from Quebec. Canada exists because, as a founding partner, Quebec made it happen.

There are other ways in which our world has very clearly changed. It was a central premise of the post-Roosevelt era that a period of expansive growth would benefit everyone, most particularly those with the lowest incomes. The political assumption was that broad social insurance was necessary to protect everyone, because everyone was equally vulnerable. If most people feel they are one pay-cheque away from poverty, they will be looking for the greatest amount of protection. Solidarity is of greater value, because the commitment to social spending is not done out of generosity or charity. It is done out of a sense of self-interest. It is the natural, highly personal response to Hillel's first question: "If I am not for myself, who is for me?"

In what I have called the first chapter of the post-war period, this solidarity was reflected in both the economy and the social programmes of the Lester Pearson era. This was the reality best described in the memorable phrase of President John Kennedy: "the rising tide lifts all boats." A largely male, white, industrial workforce saw its incomes rise steadily from 1945 to 1970. The business cycle was not abolished, but even allowing for downturns and recessions, there was an undeniable steadiness to the improvement in pay, fringe benefits, and job security.

It was the confidence in the permanence of this improvement in the standard of living of ordinary people that made the Pearson reforms possible. We have now seen how fragile these reforms in fact were, and some of the reasons for the changing role and capacity of governments. We are, of course, a more affluent society than we were in 1970. But we are also a more unequal one. And, as we have seen, this inequality has in recent years been exacerbated by the deliberate decisions of governments.

This inequality is felt in a number of ways. Everyone by now should be familiar with the basic statistics: the top fifth has moved farther ahead; the bottom fifth has fallen farther behind. More importantly, the top 60 per cent of the population is moving forward faster than the lower forty. This has the most important political consequences.

Well-paid industrial jobs are declining in importance. They are being replaced by a myriad of positions in the service sector, which covers a very broad range. Some are low-paid, part-time, the "McJobs" that have helped to define the so-called "generation X" in our collective minds. The most marginal of these are the greatest part-timers of them all, the "squeegee kids" who will wash your car windshield at every traffic stop in our cities in exchange for whatever kindness you may bestow. But, as every lawyer and investment banker knows, not every service job is marginal or low-paid. More seriously, the information economy depends on millions of skilled workers for its growth. People who fail to understand the essential dynamism of the technology around us ask questions like "What will be the jobs of the future?" The answer is a simple "No one really knows," because the pace of change is such that neither technologies nor the companies that will create them are permanent or predictable.

The global economy has brought with it great advantages for some and massive insecurity for others. The rising tide lifts many yachts, and strong cruising boats even more so. Other, smaller craft are swamped. Older workers tend to do better than younger; whites better than non-whites; men better than women; above all, the educated and skilled do much better than those with less formal schooling.

The growing inequality is even expressed in the statistics around working time: people with good work are working longer hours, and making more money as a result. The growth in part-time work since the 1970s has been explosive. Some of it is voluntary, and expresses the changing nature of family and other commitments. But much of it is involuntary, and reflects the imbalance between the haves and the have-nots.

The basis of most populism is that someone else, some evil external force, is to blame for this phenomenon. Life is more complex. We have already seen that it is technological change itself which is at the core of the drive to globalization, and that the organization and control of this technology lies outside the hands of the nation-state. Similarly, more open economies, the absence of capital controls, and the increasingly international strategies of companies all set limits on what governments can do, and how they can tax and regulate.

The causes of the growing inequality are many. They partly reflect the impact of new technologies and globalization. They also have to do with changing working conditions, and dramatic shifts in the workforce itself. When we come to turn to some proposed solutions, we shall see that it is not as easy as it first appears to craft answers.

But it is not true that we are powerless to effect some solutions. Whether dealing with the growing inequality we see around us every day, with all its potential for civil unease, and even unrest, or coming to terms with a world that may be a village in some senses but most definitely is not in terms of the vast differences between us, we face choices that are both moral and political.

And so we come to the second of Hillel's questions: "But if I am only for myself, what am I?" Self-interest is a necessary but hardly a sufficient basis for a decent society. We live in more than a market-place, and so it is to this second question, the call of solidarity, that we must now turn.

CHAPTER FIVE

The Second Question:
Charity and Welfare—The
Old Debate Is New Again

THE KEY ASSUMPTION OF CLASSICAL LIBERAL thought—what today would be dubbed the "neo-conservative agenda"—was that private decisions on their own would produce the best possible social and economic result. Michael Ignatieff, one of the most articulate defenders of liberal thinking today, rightly points out that what distinguishes liberalism from "possessive individualism" is its appeal to empathy. Rabbi Hillel's second question—"But if I am only for myself, what am I?"—makes the same point. The pursuit of self-interest is a necessary precondition for a decent social order, but a good society requires more. It requires the ways and means for empathy and solidarity to be reflected in everyday life.

Simply put, every successful society will need to

recognize and reward individual success as well as demonstrating an organized capacity for social compassion. The U.S. and Thatcherite Britain are countries that meet the first condition. They fail the second. There are innumerable examples of countries that have pursued compassion on the assumption that prosperity would always be there, and ended up failing both tests. Some, like Holland and Sweden, have begun to make the structural changes required to get things back on track. Others have found it more difficult, and more painful.

A successful politics will understand that pursuing both prosperity and the public interest—finding the right answer to Hillel's first two questions—is not easy. But that is the challenge that must be met.

The right's answer to the pursuit of compassion is that private charity alone will bridge the gap between rich and poor, between the successful and the disadvantaged.

The standard argument is clear: scarcity is the common lot of humankind. The capitalist market system, based on the self-interest of individuals and the natural right of the individual to private appropriation, would produce the most efficient economy, the best distribution of wealth, and the fairest treatment of the individual. These arguments are made with equal force today, although they admittedly have to contend with a public sector larger than anything contemplated in the nineteenth century. It is important to deal with them factually so they can finally be put to rest.

The major cuts in federal and provincial transfers to social service agencies, health care, education, and social housing over the past several years have not been matched by an explosion in private giving. Nor will they ever be.

Cuts have increased both inequality and poverty, and they will continue to do so unless they are reversed. It is not simply that the incomes of the poorest Canadians have been cut. This we know. It is also that the budgets of those agencies whose mission it is to help low-income Canadians have been slashed at the same time. People with little income rely on public institutions to provide them with the services they need. Wealthier people can buy private health care, private education, and private home nursing. But a general decline in public goods in these areas is an assault on equality and common citizenship.

Can private philanthropy possibly fill the gap? Can voluntarism make the critical difference where tax-based support has simply disappeared? The answer, on the evidence, is clearly "no."

According to the latest statistics, there are fewer people making charitable donations than in the early 1990s—just over a quarter of income-tax filers, for a total of $3.5 billion. This is not surprising, given the recession of the early 1990s. But it is a sad fact that the average donation of those who gave was less in

1995, in constant dollars, than in 1984 ($450 as opposed to $458).

What is remarkable is the continuing stinginess of Canadian corporations, whose level of giving for charities stood at 0.88 per cent of pre-tax profits in 1971 and at 0.77 per cent in 1995.

In this factual context, the extent of corporate self-congratulation over giving stands in remarkable contrast to the amount that is given. The other difficulty is that companies increasingly pursue charitable giving as an extension of their corporate profile. Helping low-income, homeless people is less media positive than helping a hospital or university. The result is that, even in the world of charity, those who need the most get the least.

My point is not to discourage private philanthropy. Quite the contrary. A decent society wants to encourage an individual sense of giving and social engagement, however and whenever it can. It is rather that the free market argument that private giving is an adequate substitute for an ever-diminishing state is an illusion. It can only be an addition, a necessary addition, but just that and no more.

Something else happens in a society which is reduced to constantly entreating rich people to give a little more money away. We celebrate wealth accumulation at the expense of other worthwhile activities: our universities and hospitals dedicate buildings, streets, Chairs, and scholarships to the inheritors of fortunes rather than to poets, musicians, and artists.

They will protest that they must. Religious and charitable organizations fall over themselves to reward as "Men of the Year" or "People of Achievement" people who have succeeded in the endeavours of business and finance, in the hope that this recognition will be matched by a generous gift. We're in danger of losing our balance and sense of proportion. This adulation of wealthy people is unseemly. Wealth need not be despised or ignored. But it should not be alone in being rewarded and celebrated.

Those who are really concerned about homelessness, the growing gap between rich and poor, and the emergence of a growing underclass in Canada cannot, if they are serious, simply look to private giving if they want to make any significant contribution to those in need. They have to look elsewhere, to public policy, to which we shall now turn.

Canada's welfare state, while badly weakened, is hardly penniless. We have, over the years, spent a great deal of public money in sustaining the public good. My argument is that we need to spend it more wisely.

Looking at the expenditure of the whole public sector (federal government, provinces, municipalities) together, we spend billions on health, pensions, unemployment insurance benefits, welfare, support for the vulnerable, and education. Looking at the regulation side of the ledger, governments of differing stripes and philosophy have made it harder (or easier) to organize a union, get paid a minimum wage, have a safe workplace, get reasonable vacation pay or maternity leave, and fight discrimination.

Why is there such a strong sense that these approaches are inadequate? The first answer is because there are visible signs that the welfare-state roof is leaking. Youth unemployment is much too high. Well over 10 per cent of the Canadian population is on unemployment insurance or welfare. Hospital care seems threatened. Yet the age-old social democratic answer of "spend more money" is less popular than it was, if only because the public instinctively understands that this means higher taxes.

Government debts have grown to the point where they risk preventing a capacity for innovation in the public sector itself. And not just governments have become highly leveraged—individuals and companies as well have been going heavily into debt in order to maintain their standard of living. The gap between rich and poor has widened. Those able to participate fully and effectively in the global economy have done well. Those whose lack of necessary skill, education, and wealth prevent them from climbing on the job escalator—both young and middle-aged—face a future on the very margins of society. These are not exclusively Canadian problems. They are faced, in varying degrees, by every industrial country. But there can now be no statistical doubt that this rising tide of globalization is not lifting all boats.

The latest evidence is that real incomes for most

Canadians fell by 8 per cent in the 1990s, and that the percentage of Canadians living in poverty increased by a quarter. Incomes of racial minorities are 15 per cent below the national average. Aboriginal incomes are 34 per cent lower than the Canadian average. While the number of families increased 6 per cent during 1990–1995, the number of low-income families increased 32 per cent. In Toronto alone, 15 per cent of households were classified as low-income in 1990; that number reached 21.1 per cent by 1995. The average income in Toronto declined a full 10 per cent. Half the one-parent families headed up by women are now described as low-income; a quarter of male-led single-parent families are poor.

Like sailors, we cannot change the weather or the direction of the wind. But we can change the direction of our sails.

The story of the last twenty-five years is one where all Western societies have had to come to terms with slower growth, rapid technological and social change, and a deeper understanding of the connection between our economic and political institutions and prosperity.

There are a few on the left who still insist that sovereign governments, committed to greater equality of outcomes, can use the state to steer the economy and society in the direction the elected majority wants. But in many cases, that would mean higher taxes, bigger governments, more intervention, more social engineering, more laws, and more regulation.

Fortunately this formula, in its classic form, no longer has much appeal.

A much bigger problem is the ideological fixation of the right. The right-wing "revolutionaries," as they call themselves in Ontario, are misguided and dangerous. They govern in the name of a theory, and in a spirit of ideological fervour. They prefer to tear everything down and "start all over again." They start from the premise that "nothing is working." They have no respect for what has gone before, or been tried before. In the case of metropolitan government, for example, they have reached the curious conclusion that creating a single centralized bureaucracy and administration for 2.5 million people and then downloading and off-loading services like housing, welfare, and long-term health care will save money and reduce the tax burden.

It will do no such thing. It will produce more costs, higher property taxes and service charges, and more inequality. Unless the plan is drastically changed, it will not produce deep prosperity or a growth which is widely shared.

The right wants "government" smaller, ignoring the fact that the vast majority of the taxes we pay as Canadians go to health care, education, pensions and income support, as well as policing, health and safety, and environmental regulation, and not to government bureaucracy itself. The right rarely has the courage to say "We want to cut health, education, and pensions."

They mouth the cliché that "Government is the problem," and claim that once we are freed from the impossible burden of taxation, the clutches of unions, and the dead hand of inspection and regulation, all will be well.

The price for this forced march is high. Health, education, and public services suffer. The wealthy avoid the cuts by purchasing their own services in the market-place. As the quality of services declines, public confidence is further eroded. Human nature being what it is, everyone aspires to jump the queue: the rat race turns us all into bigger and better rats.

The principle of trust also speaks to the importance of partnership between all the players in the modern economy. We are, as a country, profoundly reliant on our continuing access to world markets. We always have been, but never more so than today. Nearly half our GDP depends on exports—up from 35 per cent only five years ago. We cannot afford low wages and corresponding long strikes, deep divisions, inefficiency, or a disregard for productivity.

Old models of irreconcilable divisions between "us" and "them" have to be thrown away. Through their pension plans both public and private, working people have a profound stake in the health of our economy. Quebec's Solidarity Fund—an investment vehicle controlled by Quebec unions themselves—is an important model for the rest of the country and is a demonstration of what can only be called "democratic capitalism." These lessons were applied in the reconstruction of Ontario's economy in the 1990s to some real effect.

Our commitment to the democratic values of community and solidarity necessarily affects the nature of our economy, but it does not exist in mid-air, independent of the economy. Governments should not do too little. But we do pay a price when they try to do too much. We have all had to learn the lesson that there are more good ideas than there is money. Neither envy nor greed are values likely to lead to the practical social and economic policy that will produce both prosperity and the public good.

There is no one big ideological "answer." But there are better approaches. Devolve as much power to local governments as possible, but insist on co-ordination. And governments, in turn, should devolve as much power to the community as possible. Governments steer better than they row. Focus whatever tax relief can be afforded on the lowest paid, and give people every incentive to earn, work, and learn. Reduce the work week and working time. Reward patient capital. Discourage speculation if it re-emerges. Don't punish success, but give every incentive for private generosity. Don't reduce taxes to the point where the public sector can no longer provide decent health care, vital infrastructure investment, and education. Canada can ensure its competitive advantage through its strengths in health care, infrastructure investment, and education.

The left's answer to welfare reform has been widely perceived as simply giving people who are not working more money to stay at home. This approach created a reaction from working families who then determined that their taxes were simply being used to subsidize idleness. This happened in the U.S., in the U.K., and now in Canada. It has changed the welfare debate.

Social democracy needs to put work and education back at the centre of its commitment to income support. Of course, we need to avoid the frenzy to punish the victim that has for centuries been at the heart of the right's approach. Writing seventy years ago, Sidney and Beatrice Webb described how the English Poor Law was slowly evolving from what they called a "Framework of Repression" to a "Framework of Prevention." We do not seem to have advanced very far along that road.

We are told by the Webbs that what forced a change in the poor law in 1834 was a "spectacular increase" in expenditure on the poor paid for by a variety of local taxes:

> the financial burden was universally felt to be crushing; largely because of its inequitable and oppressive and local incidence. For the rates were exacted, not from those who were receiving the rapidly rising rents, royalties and profits, but in accordance with the Elizabethan legislation, from every occupier of lands, houses, titles inappropriate, or

appropriations of titles, coal mines and selectable "underwoods."[1]

The industrial revolution's growing middle class resented a tax increase on top of a stagnating post-Napoleonic War economy. The result was a new law in the 1830s which limited public support for the poor in a drastic fashion, and required that if able-bodied paupers and their families wanted relief, they would have to go to the poor house to get it.

The 1834 report has passages that might bring tears of joy to the eyes of even a Mike Harris and his minions. Take this account of what would happen once the principle of no relief outside the workhouse was applied:

> New life, new energy is infused into the constitution of the pauper, he is aroused like one from sleep, his relation with all his neighbours, high and low, is changed; he surveys his former employers with new eyes. He begs a job—he will not take a denial—he discovers that everyone wants something to be done. He desires to make up this man's hedges, to clear out another's ditches, to grub stumps out of hedgerows for a third; nothing can escape his eye, and he is ready to turn his hand to anything.[2]

The premise that it is welfare alone that makes people lazy, that unemployment is voluntary, that idleness is a condition perpetuated by "hand-outs" from government is still very much part of the welfare debate in Canada. It is not a new idea and it is not common sense.

Yet it is equally hard to deny that the very existence of unemployment insurance and welfare in turn affects behaviour. We have created what one economist has called the "quicksand effect," by which he means that the very act of income support for people fully capable of working on a sustained, institutionalized basis creates its own problems. Ever since the beginning of this century it has been an ever-more widely accepted truth that unemployment is more a reflection of a badly working economy than of an inadequate character. We should certainly hold on to that insight. Yet social democrats have to come to terms with the renewed force of the conservative argument that a complete package of entitlements with few reciprocal responsibilities on the part of the individual creates its own "moral hazard."

Social democracy must now make welfare reform its own issue. Dependency is not a good thing. It is a problem. Social democracy is about reciprocal rights and responsibilities. It is about what we owe each other. This solidarity is not a one-way street, a manifesto of state largesse with no sense of contract in return.

John Richards has written recently on this subject in his book *Retooling the Welfare State.*[3] It is unfortunate that the positive side of his argument has been lost in his rhetorical excess. When Richards argues that social democrats have to take the pledge on debts and deficits and learn from Tony Blair and also from Saskatchewan, I agree with him entirely.

When he argues that income support should be targeted broadly to working people, and that the federal and provincial income tax systems should be geared much more to work, he is right. There are still disincentives because of a lack of support for home care, child care, training, drug costs, and transportation for people seeking to get off welfare and return to the workforce. These should end. People making less than $40,000 per year should be paying less in taxation than they are today, and should have every encouragement and incentive to work. More people should be taken off the income-tax rolls entirely.

But Richards is very wrong about the relationship between the modern state and the family. He actually comes close to arguing that while single mothers should be out working, it would be better if women in two-parent families were encouraged to stay at home. This is the "nanny state" with a vengeance.

Of course it would be nice if women and men stayed together. But the state does not really re-enforce family values if it pretends the world has not changed as much as it has. The increase in the rate of divorce and family breakdown is a secular trend that "do-gooding" governments cannot change. It is the result of thousands of private decisions, wrought of emotions and tragedies the state cannot comprehend, and should not try to interfere with. And the state has no business dictating to women who should work and who should not.

The enthusiasm for work and welfare reform · 103 · should not be intrusive. The parents of children should be expected by their fellow citizens to care for them in the context of a society that supports that care and that understands the variety and diversity of family life. Those who evade their family obligations and support payments should be made to pay. Women who choose to work should be able to know that child care will be available and affordable. There should be incentives to work, to learn, and to train, but the child benefit should be broadly distributed, and not just available to people on welfare or income support.

What about workfare? It has become a bumper sticker, a slogan. Yet at its extreme it is really just a return to the Poor Law philosophy of 1834. It is reasonable to expect people to take the opportunity to learn and retrain when faced with long periods of unemployment. But the punitive, disciplinarian tone of the Victorian workhouse should not be revived. The "framework of repression" should be dismantled for all time. Governments should remove any tax disincentives against hiring, which means that the enthusiasm for payroll taxes has to be challenged. Employers need to be encouraged to provide jobs and training, even if it means subsidizing employment and education in the workplace. Workers should be allowed to join unions, and to work together to improve their lives.

There is a distinctly Dickensian feel to the neo-conservative solutions. They are punitive, which is precisely why social democracy has to challenge the current direction of right-wing thinking and practice. The challenge cannot be of the "something for nothing" variety. This will never be accepted by the majority of working people, and the longer the left only talks the language of grievance and entitlement, the longer it will remain marginal to the current debate.

The idea of reciprocity extends farther. The age of transfers without responsibilities is clearly diminishing for governments as well as individuals, and the federal government can do a great deal through tax policy to encourage the changes that are needed. The age of reliable federal transfers to provinces for health, education, and social assistance is over. This experience has been matched in virtually every province by provincial cuts in general transfers to boards, agencies, and municipalities.

Overlapping transfers create real problems both for public finance and for programme accountability and innovation.

Nothing demonstrates this more clearly than the response of Ontario Premier Mike Harris to Paul Martin's 1998 federal budget: he attacked it because it did not transfer more money back to Ontario for health care and education. This from a government that has cut billions from those very same budgets, and borrowed to pay for a tax cut that rewards the better-off. Mr. Harris is a wolf in wolf's clothing: he will fool no one with his protestations.

The purpose of transfers from one level of government to another should mainly be to equalize opportunity across the country or province. Citizens should know which level of government is accountable for which expenditure, and there should be as little mixed jurisdiction as possible.

Ottawa is in a much weakened position to enforce unilaterally any so-called "national standards" in areas of provincial jurisdiction, like health care. If they don't pay the piper, they have no right to call the tune. The recent provincial agreement in Saskatoon is an inevitable reflection of the shift in relative fiscal power between the provinces and the federal government.

What will hold the country together in this age of greater regionalism is the political will to share standards, values, and enforcement. There will be an advantage to local innovation, which is what federalism at its best is supposed to be all about. At the same time, the principle of equalization (which is actually enshrined in the constitution) should ensure a relative equality of resources and taxing power.

If directing federal spending into an elaborate web of shared transfers is no longer a real option for the national government, the advantage of a single federal income tax should ensure that the federal government focuses its attention on transfers to individuals through the tax system. There is much still to do to ensure that the income-tax system provides all the

incentives it can to encourage people to return to work and to keep working. The child tax benefit which the provinces and the federal government agreed to in 1996 (and which was proposed by Ontario in 1993) is a very modest start to what should be a more intelligent way to ensure solidarity: all lower-income families with children would receive income-based support through the tax system from Ottawa. The provinces and the federal government would then intertwine social assistance with employment insurance to ensure a co-ordinated approach to training, child care, and return to work. The disabled and those truly unable to work (or train or learn) would receive a disability pension, where, again, the existing Canada Pension and provincial programmes would be linked, and ultimately combined.

Some of this argument will make some traditional social democrats queasy. But it is hard to see anything particularly noble about a welfare and social security system that gives people a cheque if they make their way to the right wicket, and then tells them to go away. There is surely something wrong if the first cheque a young person receives when he or she leaves home is a welfare cheque. Getting people back to work and off welfare is not a right-wing objective, it is a common goal. It is also not just part of the "corporate agenda."

The irony, of course, is that the shift to a more activist approach was started in recent years by social democratic governments. Ontario, British Columbia, and Saskatchewan all expanded child care and adult education. They all linked return to the labour market with better training. They lacked the punitive edge of more conservative governments across North America, but that is as it should be.

The Second Question: Health, Education, and the Democratic Economy

THE EXTENSION OF PUBLIC, TAX-BASED SUPPORT for health care and education are rightly seen as the bedrock of modern solidarity. The fact that they are supposed to be accessible is what gives democracy more than just a formal meaning. Yet the current controversies about health and education are a real reflection of difficult choices. The status quo is not good enough, and it is not sustainable. We have to overcome the sense that the welfare state is a completed citadel which only requires a stout defence. Social democracy needs to become comfortable again with being an advocate for change.

HEALTH

Both federal and provincial governments must also play a far more creative role in health care. The health policy debate across the country in the last ten years has not just been about money, although that has become an understandable focus. The great achievement of public hospital and health insurance, begun forty years ago, was its reflection of a profound sense among the people of Canada that access to quality care is a right, and that there would be reasonable equality of access across the country. Public health insurance is a key expression of the principle of solidarity.

But there are tremendous problems with health care in Canada. Few of us appreciate how much it costs. It is one of the main reasons taxes in Canada are higher than they are in the United States. The costs of the system are very hard to control, because we are living longer, because technologies, including drugs, are improving, and because the most significant successes of modern medicine lie not so much in finding complete cures but in turning acute illnesses into chronic ones.

Governments across the country have been enthusiastically "restructuring" health care: closing acute-care beds, shutting hospitals, reducing the amount of insurable services. This is not just a Canadian phenomenon—it is a trend across the industrialized world. Canadians might be readier to accept these cuts if they had any confidence they were part of a broader plan, and if there were not so many examples of people being denied care when they needed it, and even dying while on the waiting list. The brave new world of the "wellness model" is hard to embrace when it can't provide for those who are sick.

The health bureaucracies in each province (and in Ottawa) are also ill-equipped to provide answers to pertinent questions like, Which treatments are working? and To what effect? Doctors resent interference in their practice because they insist they know best and the doctor-patient relationship is sacred. Private insurance companies in the U.S. are much more aggressive about insisting on more attention to outcomes, although their motivation is purely financial.

The public system in Canada has not been able to respond to the deep changes underway. We have pushed back the grim reaper with stronger drugs, better living conditions, and dramatic new treatments. We have not developed enough successful strategies for long-term care, or, more accurately, we have by inaction sanctioned a two-tier health system for the major growth areas in health care: drugs, and home care for the chronically ill and ageing.

A massive injection of new public dollars without a plan in place—nationally, provincially, and locally—would be a serious mistake. But targeted new spending is required for pharma care and home care; and a common approach to funding by both Ottawa and the provinces is clearly required.

The administration of this new approach must be local. Municipal and regional governments have to assume more responsibility for co-ordinating services, within budgets that are based on population. Health-care professionals of all kinds would be expected to work in teams. The task of both provincial and federal bureaucracies, which would be dramatically downsized, would be to encourage an assessment of outcomes according to the best international standards and practices.

· 114 ·

These are not revolutionary suggestions. They build on trends already underway in almost every province, but will face opposition because they recognize that the status quo is unsustainable. Hospitals would have to be less hierarchical. Unions (including the medical associations) would have to be prepared to give up job turf, and general practitioners would no longer be paid on a fee-for-service basis. Changes in hospitals would be matched by an increase in the number of community jobs.

Health is an over-bureaucratized system. The health bureaucracy in Ottawa and every provincial capital should be broken up. Regional authorities with real budget control over health promotion, home care, public health, and hospital care should make the key local and regional decisions. Small policy units in Ottawa and the capitals could focus on broader health research, on the broad trends in care, treatment, and research that will affect care in the future.

In the first generation of medicare, governments

socialized the cost and insurance of acute medical illness by spreading the burden to taxpayers. Much more now is required: if we keep on socializing the cost without really managing the system, medicare's future is in peril. It is impossible to construct a potentially more expensive system. The cost of the collapse of medicare would not be borne by the better-off (including the unionized with benefit packages); it would hit those unable to bear the market cost of their care or their insurance. This is true today of home care and the cost of drugs. It will be true of other parts of health care if governments and citizens fail to understand that the system continues to need better management as well as better funding.

Health care needs this kind of attention and leadership. Reforms like this have already begun in Saskatchewan and British Columbia. Instead of quarrelling about money, health ministers have to come to grips with their own responsibilities.

There is still a role for Ottawa. Indeed, logic would suggest a national drug insurance plan linked to the income tax system, and an end to ten pettifogging provincial drug approval bureaucracies. The quid pro quo would be a much more limited direct federal role in a hands-on delivery programme like home care, where local adaptability makes much more sense.

EDUCATION

The one central fact about the new economy we are moving into is that learning will be at its centre. It is a world of abounding technological change with a truly global reach. We are a trading country that makes its way in the world because of our ability to make goods and perform services at prices and with a quality that compares favourably with others. We cannot afford to lose sight of this central fact. The quality of our public services and the level and constancy of support we can provide for each other depend in good measure on two things, which are of equal importance: our prosperity, which should never be despised, and on our sense of mutual obligation and justice, which in turn gives meaning and reward to our prosperity. These are not exclusive values. They reinforce each other.

Learning is at the centre of the new economy, and at the centre of our society. How can we demonstrate its importance more effectively than we do?

The 1960s began a shift in educational philosophy that needs to be re-thought. According to this view, focusing on the individual student and the quality and nature of his or her experience was more important than the substance of what was taught. Hierarchies of learning and courses were less important than the "relevance" of the material to the student. Fixed courses of study, curricula that reflected a body of knowledge certain in space and time, were discarded in favour of looser ranges or groupings of study that could be chosen, cafeteria-style, by the student. The Plowden Report, which expressed the philosophy of the 1960s in Britain, argued that schools should "allow children to be themselves and to develop in the way and at the pace appropriate to them."

The Canadian report that set the pace of change in the 1970s and beyond was the Ontario Royal Commission, the Hall-Dennis Report. It led to the abandonment of general matriculation examinations, and a revamped curriculum in the name of "child-centred learning."

There is now a growing recognition that this has produced a culture of learning with its own problems. Failure and success were harder to assess. Indeed, at one ideological extreme, the very word "failure" was not allowed to be heard. Yet it is a difficult truth that not all learning is fun. It requires discipline and steadiness of purpose, as well as imagination. There is a growing sense that we have not been challenging ourselves enough. This is what needs to change.

It is better that we start with the premise that the glass is half full. It is very hard to motivate people if we convince ourselves that everything is broken and all must be started anew. The premises of revolutionaries are dangerously self-serving. They start by arguing that the status quo is a disaster and that the world must be changed to conform with a particular theory. Whatever pain and suffering follows from the revolutionary plan is described as a "necessary adjustment," and in any event completely justified by what is described as the appalling nature of the existing situation. In the course of things, much harm is done; much damage is done to what is good and constructive in human life and human relations.

We need to be infused with a spirit of steady improvement, rather than with the need to turn the world upside down in the name of a revolution. There has already been too much catering to what is fashionable in education, and too little to the fundamentals of what we know.

In the nineteenth century, which was the first century of public education, children grew up in a world without television, movies, or radio. The book was king. Most children left school before their teenage years, and certainly not all could read, but we did achieve a great degree of basic literacy in the necessary skills of an economy rapidly shifting from its agricultural base to the factory.

The modern discussion and debate about education has to come to grips with television, computer games and the Internet. Young children coming to school for the first time will already have spent thousands of hours in front of the TV, and can be expected to spend more time watching TV every week than they spend in school. We "blame schools" for poor results, yet don't really look at the entire context in which learning is taking place. As long as parents adopt a totally passive attitude to their kids' leisure-time addiction to television and computer games, they can hardly blame schools entirely for what their children are learning.

There is no point in adopting a Luddite attitude to technology. But we can continue to insist that television perform a critical, educational role. We also have to recognize the enormous, untapped potential that new forms of interactive learning now present for children. In a few years' time, we shall no longer be referring simply to "broadcast television." It will be more a matter of our choosing programming and courses of learning that we can follow at our own pace and in our own time.

The school will become a focus for sharing knowledge, learning, and skills with the community around it. Ideally we would see the physical infrastructure of the school as a community resource, starting with pre-school children and their parents, and involving senior citizens as mentors and valued guides. Early childhood education is even more important in the age of television and the Internet than before. The addictive effect of these technologies has to be offset early on; working parents need to have their children cared for; the evidence is overwhelming that early childhood learning opportunities do an enormous amount for young children and their families. This is not "babysitting."

Parents confronted with poor test results should start demanding more from all of us, more from government, more from teachers, more from the leaders of schools. This is entirely to the good. The last thing we want is to encourage complacency or a sense that nothing can be done. Some parents will express their dissatisfaction by moving their kids out of the public system. But parents have to take the more fundamental step of demanding more of themselves and their children.

This will place the burden of leadership back on parents, students, and the teachers and principals of the individual public school. This is especially true in a time of confusion about the role and number of school boards. Yet this is entirely as it should be: the school will remain the central focus of parents' and students' lives and concerns. The principal of each school has to emerge as a stronger figure, more accountable, and in turn more capable of expecting accountability from the individual teacher and student.

Each school would be freer to set its course within the public system, with the central and regional authorities concerned with regular assessment of results according to the redesigned common curriculum. How each school gets there, and what else is done on the journey, is less important. The point is for schools that are less successful to learn from those that are more so.

The key to more successful schools is effective, fairly-compensated, well-motivated teachers. Over twenty years of political life I was increasingly struck by the fact that the professional representatives of teachers have been remarkably under-represented in the debate around the quality and performance of the public-school system. Issues of compensation, governance as it relates to job tenure, broad political issues with the government of the day: these issues have been the focus of teacher-union activity. Dealing with poor results, curriculum reform, young kids' performance in science and math, the central questions of how to improve education; here the debate has been filled by parents, by academics, by some politicians, but not as much by the organizations whose job is to advance the point of view of teachers. This is a missed opportunity, to say the least. With the predominance of the political agenda today, there is little sign that this will change, unless teachers themselves demand that it do so.

Teachers should be among the leaders of this debate, and should be the leaders of educational improvement and reform. The adversarial nature of bargaining has tended to move the focus away from education itself, and this is much to be regretted. There is nothing inevitable about this—the trend can be reversed, but it will require a change of head and heart.

At the same time, governments have to stop teacher bashing. Angry teachers can defeat governments, but ultimately this is less important than their ability to short-circuit change in the classroom and in the school, if they are persuaded that this is only way their voice can be heard. A successful improvement in our schools can only happen with the full support of the teaching profession—teachers are the key, and shifting the debate within the profession is crucial for this to happen.

The teachers face the challenge of a public that wants value for money and has heard much resistance to change but not enough positive vision. The teachers and their federations need to tell Canadians how things could be improved without spending vast new sums of money. The public needs to understand why most governments around the world are focusing more energy and attention on education. Globalization and unprecedented technological change make education and training more critical to the success of our society than ever before. Public opinion—to which governments must respond—demands quality and results.

The radical right has an agenda on public education as it does on everything else. Its central premise is to hate the status quo, and make it look and sound much worse than it is. If successful, they hope that this will lead the way to a demand for vouchers, for charter schools, for the obliteration of teachers' federations. Arguments that were on the fringe in the sixties and seventies are now part of the central ideological agenda of the government. Ironically, this radicalism will set back the cause of more modest improvement and reform. A generation of embittered and resentful teachers is no prescription for improving the quality of education.

Yet in many ways social democrats share the

dilemma facing the teachers. Too much of what one hears as a solution to the challenge is a simple "more money." Canada already spends a lot of money on education in primary and secondary schools by any international comparison. Why aren't the results better?

As in health care, while radical cuts in spending make matters worse, there is no evidence to suggest that huge increases in spending on their own would make things better. The cliché heard all around us is that "learning is for life." Like many clichés, it is true. It points to the fact that we need to focus more attention on the earliest years. A number of United Ways across North America are funding programmes with the simple title "Success by Six." This points to an important truth: life chances and learning opportunities are in many ways set before a child even gets to school. Poverty, bad housing, lousy nutrition, broken families, child physical and mental abuse: these all make their nasty contribution to a meaner and more marginal life.

Time magazine—that quintessential representative of middle-American thinking—recently devoted a special report to this issue:

> Deprived of a stimulating environment, a child's brain suffers ... "there is a time scale to brain development, and the most important year is the first," notes Frank Newman, President of the Education Commission of the states. By the age of three, a child

who is neglected or abused bears marks that, if not indelible, are exceedingly difficult to erase.[1]

We spend the vast bulk of money in the health, welfare, and education systems in the later years of life. Yet it is in the earliest years that life chances are moulded and set. Fraser Mustard, the pioneering founder of the medical school at McMaster University, whose work on the connection between science, innovation, prosperity, health, and well-being is truly groundbreaking, puts it in these terms:

> Good affordable day care (mainly good support for parents, particularly mothers and their children) or early childhood education for all sectors of society is key for a future learning society. All evidence indicates that the competence and coping skills of a population in childhood and adult life is a gradient when assessed against socio-economic markers such as income and education. This means that the biggest part of the problem is in the middle class population, although the largest proportions affected will be the children in poverty. The 7,000 infants born this week are beginning the process of wiring their brains for a lifetime that will have a large influence on their behaviour and capacity to learn throughout the rest of their lives and how they work as members of society. If society, parents and governments do not pay attention to the conditions under which this crucial and delicate process

takes place, we will all suffer the consequences starting early in the next century.[2]

These issues can be addressed, but they will require a spirit of innovation and a willingness to make a social investment. This means money as well as focus and commitment to assessing outcomes, which in turn means that not as much can be spent elsewhere. The history of public spending everywhere is that, unless checked by deliberate policy, the lion's share of spending will go to the interests of the status quo. A government committed to reform cannot simply acquiesce to what those with a vested interest want.

If we agreed to make education the key priority, the key investment, we could do much. Every child could have a computer, with access to the Internet. Every aspiring educator would have the joy of a job. Parents would know they were part of a deeply supported community endeavour. Every worker would have access to better training. A steelworker's sabbatical would be as normal as a college professor's. Learning and innovation would produce their own investment and wealth. Do we really have any other choice?

THE DEMOCRATIC, AND
SUSTAINABLE, ECONOMY

Edmund Burke referred to society as a contract between those who are living and those who are yet to be born. These words have developed a special meaning in our own time because of our propensity to consume so much of the world's resources. This generation can hardly claim to have even come close to meeting the test of environmental sustainability. The reason is simple enough: the price in terms of higher costs and job losses seems too high. The irony is that key industries like fishing and forestry show that the cost of neglect and simply going with the flow is even higher.

Ever since Rachel Carson's *Silent Spring* and the reports of the Club of Rome in the early 1970s, no reasonable person can claim ignorance of the cost of doing nothing. Yet resistance is everywhere: "no" to higher fuel costs, higher tobacco costs, or sharply higher prices for commodities which are both polluting and, in the case of fossil fuel, clearly finite. The OPEC-induced crisis of 1974–1975 created a vogue for environmental reform for a while, but this was quickly swamped by the know-nothing populism of Reagan and Thatcher.

Global warming is not a myth. Neither are urban sprawl, air pollution, water scarcity, and depletion of resources. Turning to sustainability will require a willingness to pay the price, which includes paying the prices which themselves are a necessary precondition to change consumer behaviour. Social democrats should finally recognize that people will change when they have to, and not before.

User fees for garbage bags will help reduce waste. Toll roads will encourage drivers to get out of cars and take urban transit. Higher prices for gasoline and heating fuel will encourage conservation. None of these ideas will be popular initially, but governments might be able to pursue them with greater determination if they are combined with a reduction in other taxes, particularly for the lower-paid, and an investment in public transit with lower fares. In the absence of new approaches to financing, local governments in Canada will not be able to afford significant improvement, or even healthy maintenance, of our transportation infrastructure. It is equally clear that so-called "senior" levels of government will not be transferring large blocks of funds as was their earlier practice.

Sustainability in public finances means insisting on discipline and balance; in welfare it means building more incentives to work and learn; in health care it means the shifting of resources to preventing illness and insisting on new strategies for promoting wellness; in education it means paying far more attention to young people and their families and constantly assessing how the system is really performing. For the whole of society it means developing a sense that we are leaving the world better than we found it.

The traditionally important constituencies for social democratic movements have had great difficulty sharing any enthusiasm for this agenda, because they perceive that it is only in a growing and prosperous economy that their own dreams of prosperity have any prospect of success.

This was the story behind the shift from Carter to

Reagan in the United States, the resurgence of working-class Toryism in Great Britain and increased support for the Reform Party and their ideas

among many working Canadians. "Sustainability" is not enough: Prosperity is the goal. The key is to deepen and broaden that prosperity without attacking its source.

If the environmental agenda has been problematic, it has been surpassed in controversy by the gender and race politics of the last quarter-century.

We saw at the end of chapter four that one of the undoubted effects of globalization and the technological revolution has been a dramatic shift in the workplace itself. Women have entered the workforce in unparalleled numbers. That is a permanent, secular change. Canada has also become, in its largest urban centres, a multiracial and not just a multicultural country.

Writing a generation ago, one of the deans of Canadian social science, John Porter, described in *The Vertical Mosaic* how power was distributed in Canada in a distinctly hierarchical fashion. The multicultural mosaic of which we were all so proud did not mean that power was fairly shared across the country. Porter was writing before the full impact of the feminist revolution, the shift in Canadian immigration policy, and the population explosion among the aboriginal peoples. Each of these has affected the mosaic for all time, and continues to raise important questions about how power and opportunity are shared.

Women are now participating in the workforce at nearly the same rates as men. On average, their rates of pay are lower, and they tend to be more sparsely represented at senior management levels. Corporate Canada is still predominately the preserve of the white man, although it is slightly broader ethnically than when Porter was writing in the late 1950s and early 1960s. Certainly French Canadians, Jews, and Italians are more widely represented than in previous generations.

But the power structure has been slow to include women in general, women and men of colour, aboriginals, and the disabled. This overwhelming statistical and sociological fact has given rise to an understandable demand for greater representation from these groups, and for pay and employment equity.

Few policies have aroused such a sustained, emotional attack. Traditional conservatives in Canada, as in the United States and elsewhere, have bitterly denounced the affirmative action and employment equity agendas as racist and oppressive, even in some instances comparing them to apartheid or the worst experiments in social engineering. Anyone who continues to raise questions about systemic discrimination is immediately accused of advocating political correctness and consigned to the cold. Judge Rosalie Abella's groundbreaking 1984 report, *Equality in Employment*, which documents this discrimination in the clearest fashion, now occupies pride of place not in legislation but in the archives.

There are issues here of politics and policy which have to be re-examined. The major political mistake has been to create the feeling that single-handedly this current generation of white men is going to be asked to pay the price for past discrimination. The right has been able to twist legislation so that the allegation of quotas is made and repeated over and over again loudly enough that it is believed. Add the insecurity caused by a steady increase in unemployment between 1989 and 1992 and you have a welcome audience for the anti-equity message. The net effect has been to set back the equity agenda.

But not entirely. Employers have developed a stronger sense of the changing world around them than the Tories and Reform. Even with no employment equity legislation, and with weakened pay equity laws, the old discriminatory patterns become harder to justify and sustain. Most of Canada's largest employers have had to develop internal policies for hiring, training, and promotion which reflect the spirit, if not the law, of employment equity. This voluntarism will work much more slowly.

The last twenty years have tested people's patience and goodwill. Canadians voted against free trade in 1988 but accepted it when the election gave the Tories a second term. They reluctantly went along with the consequent restructuring and downsizing, and now view all the media reports about growth and opportunity with a healthy degree of scepticism.

Many live in a world where the "economy" is benefiting but they are not.

This is what leads to the culture of resentment and exclusion: it takes a range of forms, from tax revolts to road rage. The clearest economic challenge of our time is how to deepen the prosperity that is shared by too few, how to deepen it on a sustainable basis, and how to move people to Hillel's second question. There is no point lecturing people on the need to be generous—they will be generous when they realize that it is in their self-interest to work for joint action.

Above all, we must come to terms with the fact that all our discussions of public policy have to take place in a new context: a world where globalization forces us to talk about results and comparisons.

There is no avoiding the questions "how are we doing?" and "how do we compare to others?" One of our problems, of course, is that at this point our indicators are too one-dimensional. But that is not a reason to stop assessing; it is a reason to force comparisons on the full range of outcomes and values that are important to us as citizens.

We need comparisons on health and well being, crime, educational opportunity, access to recreation and retirement. We need to be as relentless in comparing these outcomes as we are for taxes, unemployment and growth. There is no avoiding measurement. We need to make sure we're measuring the right things.

The Three Questions and the Question of Canada

THOMAS D'ARCY MCGEE, THE GREAT ADVOCATE of Confederation, once said that "federalism is a great principle that speaks to the very foundations of human nature."[1] One of Canada's great orators, McGee might simply be accused of rhetorical exaggeration. But that would miss the point that he was on to something.

He believed that a pure and simple ethnic or religious or linguistic nationalism could not bring a lasting solution to the problems of the Ireland of his birth, a view which led to his own assassination in 1868 at the hands of Fenian nationalists. Tens of thousands of deaths later, Irish discussions continue an effort to waken from a nightmare of remembered (some times real, sometimes exaggerated, sometimes imagined) grievance. McGee was right about Ireland. He also was right about Canada. McGee understood that Canada's diversity required a different kind of governance, a different public philosophy from its colonial past.

Speaking almost a hundred years earlier, in the parliamentary debate on the Quebec Act of 1774, another great Irishman, Edmund Burke, said, "When I compare the rights of human conquest with the rights of human nature, the latter are so great that I can give the former no consideration at all." Burke's truth lies at the heart of all great statecraft. Canada's emergence as a country was marked in fact by two historic encounters, the first between European settlers and aboriginal peoples (whose arrival in North America predated the Vikings, John Cabot, Jacques Cartier, and Samuel de Champlain by several thousand years), and the second between the English- and French-speaking immigrants who gradually became a majority in the new land.

Both encounters have been treated as a conquest by some, for whom the only logical conclusion is the triumph of the majority and the forced conversion and assimilation of the "losers." This view has by no means disappeared. During our most difficult confrontations, from 1837 and its aftermath to Oka and the post-referendum malaise, "conquest-style thinking" has lurked beneath the surface of many people's thoughts.

In our wiser moments we have listened to voices

like Burke and McGee. Treaties have been signed with rights to both sides. Clear limits have been placed on what any temporary majority could do. From the very origins of these first encounters we have had to learn that rights can belong to groups, as they can to individuals, and that pure and simple majority rule cannot be the only principle of a civilized political community.

After the battle of the Plains of Abraham in 1759, the British made two intelligent decisions. They decided to reconcile with both the aboriginal population of North America and the French Canadians in Quebec. There were some very profound geo-political reasons why the British decided to pass the Proclamation of 1763 and Quebec Act of 1774. They needed to solidify this part of North America, faced with all that was taking place in the American colonies. Yet it was truly remarkable that, in this period of imperial history, the British themselves would begin to understand the importance of the federal principle and the federal idea, even in the heart of the empire.

Having won a military victory in 1759, it would have been possible for the British to have insisted that those who had been conquered conform entirely to the culture, to the government, and to the way of life of the so-called conqueror. Wisdom pointed to another path, the road of reconciliation and mutual recognition.

Just as the Royal Proclamation in 1763 set the stage for one partnership, the Quebec Act of 1774 was the basis for another. The British Parliament passed a statute which gave extensive rights to the French Catholic minority in Quebec, a law which clearly recognized the distinct culture and civil society that is Quebec, within the imperial regime. *Les Canadiens,* as they were known at the time, could be loyal to their own faith, their own way of life. Burke argued correctly that a broader allegiance to the Crown was more likely to result from recognizing the distinctiveness of Quebec than from forcing it into conformity with Protestant and Anglo-Saxon principles and culture.

Throughout our history Canadians have, at our best, aspired to federalism. Whenever we have fallen by the wayside and ignored and misunderstood its principles, we have run into real trouble. One of the foundations of federalism is that it is part of human nature for one to have a range of loyalties and that to be loyal first of all to one's own hearth, to one's own home, to one's own faith, to one's own language, to one's own distinctiveness is entirely natural and indeed healthy.

If Quebecers had not been determined to preserve their language and culture, had not insisted on their own self-interest and had not pursued that self-interest with a vigour throughout their history, no one else would have done it for them. This question extends not only to the issue of Quebec, but to all the range of interests and to all the expressions of identity that we see around us in contemporary Canada. A basic human right is simply the right to be oneself, to be recognized by oneself and others for what one is. A modern constitution has to be a mirror in which people see themselves. The feminist revolution of the last twenty-five years, the movement for multicultural and multiracial recognition, the movement for gay rights are all expressions of people asserting their rights to be themselves and to be recognized for who they are.

It is now fashionable to designate "identity politics" as divisive and trivial. This misses the crucial point that there is a difference between identity as an essential first step and identity as the be-all and end-all. The assertion of personality and separate identity is the first step to the growth of the individual child. But if development stops there, we wind up with a pretty outrageous adult. The same is true in the life of the community. The discovery of the self is a vital and liberating first step. But the self then has to confront and recognize the other. And learning to live with the other while being true to ourselves is what federalism is all about.

The days prior to Confederation in 1867 were both a time of the country coming apart and a time of the country coming together. The tensions in the communities around Toronto and Montreal that led to the rebellions of 1837 were in part about how much popular government the elites were prepared to allow. They were also about the extent to which the distinct personality of French-speaking Canada was going to be allowed to survive. Britain's initial answer was to ask Lord Durham to investigate what appeared to be a complete unravelling in the colonies. While in English Canada we celebrate Lord Durham as the father

of "responsible government," it is crucial to realize that in Quebec, and more broadly in French Canada, Lord Durham is seen as somebody who attempted to undermine and indeed destroy the integrity and the identity of Quebec culture. A simple reading of his report explains the problem:

> I entertain no doubts as to the national character which must be given to Lower Canada; it must be that of the British Empire; that of the majority of the population of British America; that of the great race which must, in the lapse of no long period of time, be predominant over the whole North American Continent. Without effecting the change so rapidly or so roughly as to shock the feelings and trample on the welfare of existing generations, it must henceforth be the first and steady purpose of the British Government to establish an English population, with English laws and language, in this Province, and to trust its governance to none but a decidedly English legislature.[2]

The prejudices of his own time, nationality, and class led Durham down a mean path:

> The French Canadians, on the other hand, are but the remains of an ancient colonization, and are and ever

must be isolated in the midst of an Anglo-Saxon world.... it would appear, that the great mass of the French Canadians are doomed, in some measure, to occupy an inferior position, and to be dependent on the English for employment. The evils of poverty and dependence would merely be aggravated in a ten-fold degree, by a spirit of jealous and resentful national- ity, which should separate the working class of the community from the possessors of wealth and employers of labour... there can hardly be conceived a nationality more destitute of all that can invigorate and elevate a people, than that which is exhibited by the descendants of the French in Lower Canada, owing to their retaining their peculiar language and manners. They are a people with no history, and no literature.[3]

Durham went back to England in 1840. He left Canada a completely unworkable legacy. For twenty-seven years, we debated in Upper Canada and Lower Canada what new institutional forum would deal with the impossibility Lord Durham had established.

While there were many in the English elites in Toronto and Montreal who shared Durham's preju- dice, political leaders quickly emerged who believed in a very different kind of reality. William Lyon Mackenzie and Louis-Joseph Papineau were mar- ginalized by the severity and drama of their defeat in 1837, but Robert Baldwin and Louis-Hippolyte Lafontaine soon after became the first key exponents of the idea of real partnership between the English and French communities within a single country.

Their two administrations in the 1840s can be said to have changed Canada for all time. They successfully buried Durham's idea of assimilation. They established irrevocably that Canadian governments depended on the confidence of the people, and not on the whim of either the governor or London.

As Baldwin put it:

> Our objects are open and avowed. We seek no concealment, for we have nothing to conceal ... we want not only the Constitution, but as regards the administration of our local affairs, the whole Constitution and nothing but the Constitution. By the Constitution the Ministers of the Crown are responsible to Parliament for appointments to office as well as for every other act of the Government.[4]

Baldwin also understood that the implication of this responsibility was the partnership between French and English. If the Canadian legislature reflected this duality, its government could do no less. Hence the remarkable partnership with Lafontaine, which even extended to the two reformers each running successfully for office in the other's political stronghold, Baldwin in Rimouski and Lafontaine in York.

The federal idea in Canada owes precisely nothing to Durham and everything to Baldwin and Lafontaine and their successors. Durham remains a whipping post for nationalists in Quebec, who conveniently ignore the fact that he wasn't a Canadian and his governing structure was repudiated. When Lafontaine retired from politics in 1851, he said:

> I have said that the union was intended to annihilate the French Canadians. But the result has been very different. The author of the union was mistaken. He wished to degrade one race among our citizens, but the facts have shown that both races among us stand upon the same footing.[5]

The federal idea grew in the 1840s, and eventually even the Ontario Reform leader George Brown had to succumb to the logic of its approach. He came to understand that for "Canada West" to have its personality, Quebec would have to be granted hers. Perhaps even Preston Manning will find the same truth.

Canada has been an exercise in a most wonderful kind of empiricism in which we have come upon political solutions that have allowed us to interpret what is happening in different and, indeed, opposing ways. Sir John A. Macdonald wrote a famous letter to a gentleman by the name of M.C. Cameron, a hard-line Tory very much opposed to federalism:

> My dear Cameron . . . As to things political I must try to discuss the federation scheme with you. I'm satisfied that we've hit upon the only practical plan.

I do not mean to say the best plan . . . We've avoided exciting local prejudice against the scheme by protecting local interests and, at the same time, have raised a strong central government. If the confederation goes on you, if spared the ordinary age of man, will see both local parliaments and governments absorbed in the general power. This is as plain to me as if I saw it accomplished now. Of course, it does not do to adopt that point of view in discussing this subject in lower Canada.[6]

Macdonald was the master of ambiguity. He believed very strongly in the importance of a strong central government. Indeed he was one of those who believed that the local governments, as he called them, would eventually become less and less important. He was a reluctant federalist who understood that compromise was necessary and essential in order to achieve what was required in political terms in 1867.

Confederation has usually been thought of as a coming-together. This misses the point which was best described by Sir Étienne Taché, a leading Quebec politician of the day:

If a Federal Union were obtained it would be tantamount to a separation of the provinces, and Lower Canada would thereby preserve its autonomy together with all the institutions it held so dear, and over which they could exercise the watchfulness and surveillance necessary to preserve them unimpaired.[7]

"Events stronger than advocacy; events stronger than
men" (to borrow Thomas D'Arcy McGee's words)
produced the drive to federal union. But it was not,
on any terms, a drive to a unitary state. Quebec could
best "be for itself" within a federal Canada.

It took twenty-five or thirty years after Confederation for the notion of a mature federalism to emerge
more clearly in the law and politics of Canada. W.L.M.
Kennedy, the dean of Canada's constitutional lawyers
some seventy years ago, pointed out that by about
1890 it had been clearly established that the genius of
Canadian federalism was that the central government,
as the British Privy Council held, was sovereign in
areas that were assigned to it, but the provinces were
equally sovereign in the areas that had been assigned
to them. To quote from a Privy Council decision just
before the first Premiers' Conference:

> The object of the Act was neither to weld the
> provinces into one, nor to subordinate provincial
> governments to a central authority, but to create a
> federal government in which they should all be
> represented, entrusted with the exclusive administration of affairs in which they had a common
> interest, each province retaining its independence
> and autonomy.[8]

Those who are advocating the break-up of the country would have us believe that Canada is scarcely a federation at all and that the federal principle means

relatively little. They would argue that there is a doctrine called sovereignty which is absolute and which has no limits or boundaries. Yet the history, constitution, and institutions of Canada as well as what Burke would call the rights of human nature, point to a very different reality. Federalism means quite simply that some governments are sovereign in some areas, others are sovereign in other areas, and these sovereignties are not absolute; they are limited, limited by law, limited by circumstance, limited by the rights of human nature itself.

In writing his brilliant book *The Age of Paradox*, Charles Handy of the London Business School emphasizes this deeper meaning of federalism:

> Federalism is an old idea, but its time may have come again because it matches paradox with paradox. Federalism seeks to be both big in some things and small in others. It aims to be local in its appeal and in many of its decisions, but national or even global in its scope. It endeavours to maximize independence; to encourage difference, but within limits; it needs to maintain a strong centre, but one devoted to the service of the parts; it can, and should, be led from that centre but has to be managed by the parts. There is room in federalism for the small to influence the mighty, and for individuals to flex their muscles.[9]

Handy also reminds us of the difference between a confederation and a federation:

> Much of the confusion and difficulty arises from a
> misunderstanding of what federalism is. A confeder-
> ation, for example, is not the same thing as a feder-
> ation. A confederation is an alliance of interested
> parties who agree to do some things together. It is
> a mechanism for mutual advantage. There is no rea-
> son for sacrifice or trade-offs or compromise unless
> it is very obviously in one's own interest. A confed-
> eration is not an organization that is going any-
> where, because there is no mechanism or will to
> decide what that anywhere might be. The Confeder-
> ation of Independent States, which replaced the
> Soviet Union confederation, is a thing of sentiment
> and language, not a real organization. These are not
> the stuff of federalism. Confederations adapt when
> they have to, usually too late. They do not lead, nor
> do they build. They are organizations of expediency,
> not of common purpose.
>
> The key concepts in federalism are twin citizen-
> ship and subsidiarity. They are old ideas, re-invented
> for today's world.[10]

Canada needs common institutions to advance our common purpose. That is the truth Lucien Bouchard fails to see: he insists that a new partnership will bring a "win" for Quebec. This is not a zero-sum game. The centre has to be strong enough to do its job. That does not mean a big or over-bureaucratized centre. It does mean a continuing capacity to lead.

There are a range of sovereignties. We are discovering now how difficult it is to deal with the questions of aboriginal self-government. Various sovereignties compete for our loyalty. When we talk, for example, about rights of self-determination, are these rights absolute? How can they be? How can we speak of these rights in an absolute sense? We cannot.

These rights are not absolute. They are subject to circumstance. We hear the question: "Is there an absolute right to self-determination for Quebec?" An absolute right? No. There are no absolute rights. There are rights which are comparable to others. That is the issue to which we must now address ourselves. "But if I am only for myself," to return to the Rabbi's second question, "what am I?" Here again, Canada's discovery of the federal principle, something in a sense we have had to work our way towards, was born of the simple fact that none of us is completely sovereign. We do not live in a world in which we can say we have the free and absolute powers to do x, y, or z, either as individuals or as groups. That's why Hillel's second question is equally relevant not only to our historical experience, but to where we must go in the future. If it is true and good Canadian law (and it is) that no sovereignty in Canada is absolute, then the provincial governments are not derivative of the federal government, provincial powers are not subordinate to the federal power, and federal power is not subordinate to the provinces on certain matters. There are competing claims to our loyalty.

The force of these arguments has been reinforced in the thoughtful unanimous opinion of the Supreme Court of Canada on the Quebec Secession Reference. The judges put it this way:

> The significance of the adoption of a federal form of government cannot be exaggerated. Without it, neither the agreement of the delegates from Canada East nor that of the delegates from the maritime colonies could have been obtained.

Once accepted, the federation took on a life of its own, an existence that cannot easily be torn asunder: "The threads of a thousand acts of accommodation are the fabric of a nation."

Cutting through generations of rhetoric, the Supreme Court judgement makes refreshing reading. Quebeckers are not an oppressed people. They do not have an absolute right to self determination at the expense of other rights and obligations. Neither, on the other hand, do Canadians have the right to ignore a clear majority of Quebeckers speaking on a clear question of secession from Canada.

But Quebeckers, the Court warns, should not confuse discussions triggered by such a referendum result with independence:

No one can predict the course that such negotiations might take. The possibility that they might not lead to an agreement amongst the parties must be recognized. . . . there is a national economy and a national debt. Arguments were raised before us regarding boundary issues. These are linguistic and cultural minorities, unevenly distributed across the country, who look to the Constitution of Canada for the protection of their rights . . . Nobody seriously suggests that our national existence, seamless in so many aspects, could be effortlessly separated along what are now the provincial boundaries of Quebec.[11]

Even in the language and rhetoric of independence there is an extraordinary ambiguity. On the one hand, one asserts the absolute right to self-determination, the indivisibility of all borders of Quebec, the absolute right to have a referendum and for that referendum to be determinative of the future of Quebec by means of a simple majority. At the same time, we have this urge for partnership, and a constant use of other examples from Europe and other federations. The logic of the language of partnership leads inexorably to some expression of the federalist idea.

It is ironic that even in the rhetoric of independence there is a constant quest for partnership and for association. It is ironic because Canadian history shows it is the drive for partnership and association which produced federalism. If, through whatever folly, Canada were to break up, we would simply have to reinvent it. If Mr. Bouchard is seeking to renegotiate the nature of the partnership, the working of federal institutions, what should be federal and what should be provincial, and which sovereignties should apply in which ways, one has to ask: Why resort to the demagogic language of absolutes? Whatever our future relations, they will not be based on absolutes, or being only for ourselves. In all negotiations there will be concessions and compromises. No one ever goes into a negotiation expecting to get everything that is asked for in the beginning.

The Europeans, after all, are moving toward a kind of federalism, although they are not allowed to use the word in some jurisdictions. When you look at the Maastricht Treaty, in terms of the economic integration of Europe, it is far more specific than our own economic integration in Canada. Maastricht states very clearly the levels of deficit which each member country is going to be able to have in order to be part of the European currency system. So far as I am aware, no Canadian federal government has said to a province, "If you want to continue to participate in our currency arrangements, you're going to have to run your ship differently." As time progresses, a greater degree of co-operation on fiscal matters is to be expected. But Maastricht contemplates limits on fiscal sovereignty greater than anything currently in place in Canada.

The existence now of extra-territorial agreements like NAFTA and the World Trade Organization, which clearly limit the impact of sovereignty and restrict the ability of governments to do things they otherwise would have liked to do and been able to do at

different times in history, speaks to the reality that absolute sovereignty is an idea of another time and place. It is also not practical, given the nature of the Canadian political community, because of the balance that had to be struck in 1867 and because the need for that balance is as real today as it was at that time.

There is a significant English-language minority in the province of Quebec, and in the rest of Canada there is a significant French-language minority, particularly in the provinces of New Brunswick and Ontario. There is a compelling need for the interests of the minorities to be respected across the country. And just as there was a practical arrangement worked out at Meech and Charlottetown, which led to a recognition that these rights would be protected, any future arrangement will have to do the same. At our worst moments we have ignored that principle. There have always been voices in English Canada and French Canada who have felt that the rights of majorities should prevail and who have chosen (to revert to Burke's phrase) to celebrate "the rights of conquest rather than the rights of human nature." At our best in our history we have always ended up rejecting those voices, just as Burke did in 1774. We must do so again.

That isn't to say that Canada hasn't gone through periods when the principles of the central government or the powers of the federal government were held to be more important because of war or because of a particular dramatic period of change in our economy. But today Canada is highly decentralized. Provinces have a lot of jurisdiction and authority, which means there are many ways in which they can serve the people for ill or for good. The notion that provinces are, somehow, powerless little derivatives of the federal government is political and constitutional nonsense. It just isn't true.

Which brings us to Hillel's third question: "If not now, when?" There will always be excuses for delay, but complacency has helped to create the current impasse.

It is now important for two things to happen. The first thing is that we must be clearer and more emphatic across the country on the benefits and the meaning of the federalism which we have been building not just for 125 years, but, I would argue, since 1774 and the Quebec Act, which was in a sense the true beginning of a federal principle in Canada. There is a lot of misunderstanding and misinterpretation with respect to the meaning and the essence of federalism in the Province of Quebec, but there is an equal level of misunderstanding and misrepresentation in other parts of the country. Those who argue that Canada is made up of ten provinces which must be treated the same in a kind of cookie-cutter approach of total equality are arguing this in defiance of Canadian history. It might have to do with one person's theories of federalism, but we have seen the danger of governing in the name of a theory, whether it is Lord Durham's, Pierre Trudeau's, or Preston Manning's. Federalism takes different forms in different countries at different times. There is not one magic definition of federalism. There is not one way in which one can be a federalist. There is not one, and only one, federalist constitution. There are a range of constitutional possibilities. Above all, in making constitutions, we should have respect for and knowledge of the institutions, the culture, the language, and the history of our own country.

Those outside Quebec whose voices have rejected the notion of distinct society, who have shown an unwillingness to recognize Quebec's distinctiveness, are ignoring an important part of Canadian history and of Canadian reality. For generations, people outside of Quebec kept on asking the typical media question, "What does Quebec want?" I think Quebec is now entitled to say, "Well, we have a pretty good idea of what we want. We told you what that was in Meech Lake. We've given you some sense of the direction we want to go in." There's clearly a strong majority of opinion in Quebec not in favour of separation, but certainly in favour of recognizing the distinctiveness of Quebec and the particular quality of Quebec institutions. Now they are entitled to say to English Canada, "What do you want?"

The boundaries of modern-day Quebec have been agreed to within the context of the Canadian political community, not as some geographical absolute.

The native people of northern Quebec have as strong a claim to sovereignty within their own boundaries as do the people of southern Quebec. The boundaries between Upper and Lower Canada were redrawn in 1867 on the assumption of a shared political community and shared political rights within Canada. The best that can be said if Quebec were to declare unilateral political independence is that all bets would be off with respect to boundaries and borders.

And so we return to the logic of federalism. Within the Canadian tradition the word has had many different meanings and expressions. There have been those who have insisted on provincial equality with no room for official bilingualism. There have been those who have insisted on two communities, English and French, relating in two power blocs with no room for provincial diversity or multicultural reality. Few have really absorbed the meaning of aboriginal treaties or aboriginal self-government.

It was the Royal Commission on Bilingualism and Biculturalism (1963–69) over 30 years ago that pointed out the consequences of Quebec's distinctiveness and the dangers that would arise if Quebec's concerns were ignored or brushed aside:

> All that we have seen and heard has led us to the conviction that Canada is in the most critical period of its history since Confederation. We believe there is a crisis, in the sense that Canada has come to a time when decisions must be taken and developments

must occur leading either to its break-up, or to a new
set of conditions for its future existence.[12]

· 156 ·   It was this commission that coined the phrase "a
distinct society" in its discussion of the crisis and the
choices facing Canadians:

> "Overwhelming majority," "society," "nation:" what do
> they mean? They are used to describe the types of
> organization and the institutions that a rather large
> population, inspired by a common culture, has cre-
> ated for itself or has received and which it freely man-
> ages over quite a vast territory where it lives as a
> homogeneous group according to common standards
> and rules of conduct. This population has aspirations
> which are its alone, and its institutions enable it to
> fulfil them to a greater or lesser degree. In any event,
> this was the way the French speaking population of
> Quebec appeared to us.[13]

It is interesting, as a historical parenthesis, that
Premier Ernest Manning of Alberta wrote to Lester
Pearson on May 28, 1963, indicating his concern
about the Royal Commission:

> If . . . the objective is to give some form of official
> recognition to a dual English and French culture, we
> suggest this is unrealistic and impracticable and we
> doubt it would meet with any widespread public
> acceptance . . ."[14]

The terms of reference given to the Royal Commission by the government of the day spoke of an "equal partnership between two founding races." It is this idea which has been only partly accepted by Canadians outside Quebec. Aboriginal rights, provincial rights, the rights and status of those outside the pole of the two "founding races" have all combined to make the constitutional formula extraordinarily elusive.

The approach recommended by the Royal Commission was essentially that of the Meech and Charlottetown accords. It has been thwarted on many sides: by those who insist on the "strict construction" of identical provinces, like Preston Manning and Clyde Wells; by those who insist on Quebec's absolute need for independence; and, ironically, by the continuing legacy of the vision of Pierre Elliott Trudeau.

Pierre Trudeau's greatest strength has also been his greatest weakness. His political life centred on "one big thing," the demolition of Quebec nationalism, nothing more, nothing less. His greatest strength, because like many others his talents and invective were always put to best use in his *"J'accuse"* mode. His greatest weakness, because he became the prisoner of his own rhetoric, an ideologue despite himself, and curiously rigid as he tore strips off anyone who chose to disagree.

Is an accommodation with Quebec nationalism possible within the Canadian federation, or is it a silly delusion to think that some middle ground exits between Mr. Trudeau's awful symmetry and separation?

Mr. Trudeau's political life was based, essentially, on the simple notion that French Canadians should seek their full expression of citizenship in Canada itself, and not in Quebec, and that indeed the world itself should be their oyster. Patriation, the Charter, minority language rights, official bilingualism, root and branch opposition to Meech and Charlottetown were all manifestations of this "one big thing."

One can't help but feel that John A. Macdonald, Wilfrid Laurier, Mackenzie King, Louis St. Laurent, and Lester Pearson would have seen Meech and Charlottetown as worthy successors to their efforts at accommodation and compromise. It's all very well to mock those accords, as Trudeau did, as a "dog's breakfast." So was the British North America Act itself. Constitutions do not emerge perfectly formed from the brain of the philosopher king, as Mr. Trudeau himself discovered in 1980 and 1981. They are always messy processes that are easier to knock down or tear apart than they are to construct.

John A. Macdonald knew that Quebec nationalism was not about to disappear, which is why he, together with the key leadership of Upper Canada (even George Brown came around in the end) ditched the impossible effort of Lord Durham to create "one Canada." His key successors reached the same conclusion, knowing that while Canada's duality is not its only characteristic, it is certainly one of them. They learned from Macdonald's famous dictum: "Treat them as a nation and they will act as people generally do—generously. Call them a faction and they become factious."

Mr. Trudeau never did learn this.

Trudeau's hostility to Duplessis and all his works, as well as the strength of his own liberal ideology, puts him in the camp of those who see all manifestations of nationalism as a retrograde craving that progress, culture, and enlightenment would make redundant. To borrow a phrase often quoted by philosopher Isaiah Berlin, Mr. Trudeau never absorbed the wisdom of Kant's dictum that "from the crooked timber of humanity nothing straight is ever made."

In its excesses, Quebec nationalism can be offensive. But it cannot only be understood by its excesses. The need to belong to a family and a community; to treasure a language and native tongue; to value a land because it is home and nurtures common values and traditions: these are not signs of evil or weakness. Durham's vision of a culturally inferior French population disappearing in the wake of a technologically advanced English "civilization" proved to be quite wrong, precisely because of the depth of nationalist feeling in Quebec and in fact that the British North America Act of 1867 reserved significant powers for the provinces.

Writing more than a century ago, the French sociologist Ernest Renan posed the question, "What is a nation?" He pointed out that religion, race, ethnicity, and language could not be seen as the defining core of a country. They were each too restrictive and confining, too exclusive of the competing realities within any political community. He came to the simple conclusion that a nation was simply a group of people who had chosen to do great things together in the past and who choose to do them together in the future.

· 160 ·

No doubt this notion of civic nationalism is less satisfying to some than the gut appeal to race, colour, and language. But it has the advantage of assuring mutual tolerance, civic peace, and a political identity that transcends race and religion. Our best political leaders have always understood this. Our worst ones have chosen to ignore it, and have consistently led us to dead ends.

Whatever the results of the next referendum in Quebec, if there is one, certain common realities must be confronted. Political relations can always be improved, but a common currency and shared values will clearly imply co-ordination and reciprocity, as they are so clearly doing in Europe. These in turn will require common political institutions, like parliament and courts, with some powers independent of the members of the federation and common to all citizens.

A more regionalized and decentralized Canada is a growing reality, but so is the need for co-ordination. Open markets will require a limit on governments' penchant for erecting barriers to freer movement. This co-ordination will, in turn, imply reform of federal institutions.

The appointed Senate will be abolished. Our relationship with the monarchy will be reassessed. Parliament itself can usefully change. But for all these changes, an underlying truth remains: the idea of Canada, a nation and civil society with a history of partnership and solidarity, remains as strong and vibrant as we care to make it.

CHAPTER EIGHT

The Need for Politics

NO DOUBT EACH GENERATION THINKS IT HAS A unique insight into the life of the world. When I was giving a talk recently on the balance between self-interest and the needs of the community, a member of the audience pointed out a passage by the ancient historian Thucydides. When the Athenians blamed Pericles for all their misfortunes, including their suffering under the plague which had broken out, he addressed the assembled as follows:

> I am of the opinion that national greatness is more to the advantage of private citizens than any individual well-being coupled with public humiliation. A man may be personally ever so well off, and yet if his country be ruined he must be ruined with it; whereas

a flourishing commonwealth always affords chances
of salvation to unfortunate individuals. Since, then, a
state can support the misfortunes of private citizens,
while they cannot support hers, it is surely the duty
of everyone to be forward in her defense.[1]

Pericles is making a subtle but important argument. We must be forward in our defence of the priority of politics because it is in our interests to do so.
If the life of the community is impoverished, we shall
all be hurt. Like it or not, we are all in the same boat,
and the flourishing of our commonwealth "always
affords chances of salvation to unfortunate individuals." Writing just a couple of hundred years before
Hillel (and about two and a half thousand years
before us), Pericles was making this same key argument about the connection between the public good
and our own prosperity.

Politics is the art of pursuing common interests
through listening, advocacy, public persuasion, negotiation, compromise, and ultimately decision. Aristo-
tle understood that politics is, in a sense, the "master
art." It represents the pursuit of the common good,
always with the knowledge and sense that there will
be paradoxes and ambiguities. Key words are balance
and limits. We should all be reminded of Churchill's
famous comment, "Democracy is the worst possible
system of government, except for all the others."

Perhaps I can write with a slightly greater degree
of credibility now that I am what my wife calls a

"recovering politician." We all know the extent to which politics is held in ill repute. When any of us uses the words "politician" or "politics," it almost always has a sleazy connotation. I vividly recall a conversation I had with a friend who was describing a particular difficulty that he was having in an argument with his family and he said, "You know I had a choice," and I said, "What was the choice?" and he said, "Well I could either deal with it honestly and straightforwardly or I could do it politically."

The idea of politics is in need of defence. The British political scientist Bernard Crick wrote a brilliant little book by this very name, *In Defence of Politics*. The rejection of politics in favour of the so-called non-political alternatives leads to much worse consequences. Yet politics and the state are not everything. We do not want the public and political to take over our lives. We need to be reminded of what politics can and cannot do.

It might, at first blush, seem strange to lump the founder of modern conservatism, Edmund Burke, together with one of the great radical voices of the twentieth century, George Orwell. There is, indeed, much that divides them. Burke was an eighteenth century politician and a parliamentarian who believed profoundly in the importance of social and political order. An Irishman who was proud of his origins and prouder still of his association with the architects of the Whig Party in Westminster in the middle of the eighteenth century, Burke was at once a party insider and a philosopher keen to speak to first principles and the broader context of human endeavour.

George Orwell, born Eric Blair at the turn of the century, went to Eton and then went to work for the Empire in Burma. Profoundly disillusioned, he returned to England in his late twenties and decided to become a writer and a witness to the politics of the twentieth century. After tramping around England and France, experiences he wrote about in *Down and Out in Paris and London* and *The Road to Wigan Pier*, he fought in Spain on behalf of the Republicans. While in Barcelona he came to the grim realization that the Communist Party and its supporters world-wide would go to any lengths to achieve monopoly power. They would crush opposition as surely as any capitalist dictatorship. This insight produced *Homage to Catalonia*, which marked Orwell's break with the left-wing orthodoxies of the day.

He was further disillusioned by the signing of the Molotov-Ribbentrop Pact in 1939, and after working for the BBC during World War II, wrote two remarkable novels, *Animal Farm* and *1984*. George Orwell died of tuberculosis at the age of forty-six, still considering himself a socialist, certainly a profound democrat, and someone who would probably be surprised to hear himself described in the same breath as Edmund Burke.[2]

Yet there are persistent, fascinating parallels between these two great men. They were both gifted writers, probably the greatest political writers in the

English language of their age. Their capacity for irony, invective, analysis, and humour has few equals. They both recognized that politics and public life were about great questions. They both had the gift of insight into the challenges of their time. And they were both unafraid to take on the "smelly little orthodoxies" of the day on behalf of the cause of freedom and civility, regardless of party loyalties and the tyranny of conventional opinion.

Above all, they both recognized in the political revolutions that marked their lives something profoundly malicious, which had to be spoken about without fear or favour. They learned that in the making of public policy, narrow ideologies and revolutions of whole cloth were to be despised and rejected. All revolutions, in Burke's phrase, "contain in them something of evil." They produce no lasting good, and do much harm. They reject facts and experience in the name of a theory. This is something Burke knew with his very soul. It was something Orwell had to come to, seared by the experience of Spain, World War II, and the overwhelming evidence of human disaster under Stalin and Hitler.

Burke spoke compellingly of the advantages of political parties, and of their importance in the emerging constitution of Great Britain. Burke's defence of party is worth remembering today:

> When men are not acquainted with each other's principles, nor experienced in each other's talents, nor at

all practised in their mutual habitudes and disposi-
tions by joint efforts of business; no personal confidence, no friendship, no common interest subsisting
among them; it is evidently impossible that they can
act a public part with uniformity, perseverance, or
efficacy.... no men could act with effect who did not
act with confidence; and that no men could act with
confidence who were not bound together by common
opinions, common affections, and common interests.[3]

· 170 ·

Burke underlined the essential role that parties played
in the creation not only of a public philosophy, but in
the formation of government and public policy. He
described parties, in a wonderful phrase, as "these little platoons." The party which Burke helped to found
went on to effect profound change in the British constitution and in the condition of the British people.
Burke was not a reactionary. Burke believed that one
had to reform institutions in order to preserve them,
and that party was necessary to achieve reform: "No
men could act with confidence who were not bound
together by common opinions, common affections and
common interests."

It wasn't the civil service acting alone that brought
these changes, or business, or interest groups acting
by themselves. It was political parties which effected
them and which saw them through.

Consider the achievements of Burke and his group,
the great reforming administrations of William Glad-
stone and Lord Asquith in the nineteenth and early

twentieth century, the Clement Attlee Labour government between 1945 and 1951 which greatly extended the welfare state, the achievements of Franklin Roosevelt and of the Democratic majority between 1932 and 1938 which literally transformed the political, the economic, and the social condition of the people of the United States and set an example for others. Look at the recent attempted counter-revolution in the United States and even Ontario. I don't agree with the Contract for America or with the so-called common sense revolution in my own province—obviously not, it has created serious injustice for hundreds of thousands—but it cannot be denied that these have all been achieved, for better or for ill, by the political process itself.

When we look at our experiences in Canada, both provincially and federally, and we look at the periods of remarkable change and transformation in the social and political life of our country, they have been led by the political leadership of the country. They were carried out because there were dedicated, hard-working people who believed it should happen and who made it happen, and not by some process of good ideas falling from the sky.

We have considered the wisdom of the federalist idea in Canadian politics. It was not imposed by military conquest or colonial administration. It was discovered, applied, and refined by Canadian politicians. We often now hear it suggested that the way out of our current difficulties is to "take it away from the politicians," by appointing experts or trusting in the spontaneous combustion of a referendum. Nothing could be less helpful or less productive. We need to find political solutions whose momentum can best be found by leaders engaged in a serious dialogue with Canadian citizens, and proposing improvements and reforms.

The Pearson administration between 1963 and 1968 was one of the most successful, focused, reforming administrations in the history of Canada. A precarious government, it governed with a minority. But we wouldn't have the Canada Pension Plan if it had been up to the bureaucracy on its own. If it had been up to the Canadian Medical Association, we wouldn't have Medicare. If it had been up to the Canadian Chamber of Commerce, we wouldn't have the Canada Assistance Plan. None of these interest groups or people who have a variety of points of view or roles to play within the system could possibly have brought about these achievements. It required the combined political will of two political parties, the Liberals and the NDP. It required the historical leadership of Premiers Tommy Douglas and Woodrow Lloyd of Saskatchewan.

These achievements were brought about because political parties, the little platoons of loyalty bound together by common affection and common conviction, advocated, persuaded, compromised, and negotiated their way to achieving tangible, real, practical progress. That's what politics is. Compromise is not a dirty word. Compromise is a necessary part of the process, as is negotiation, as is advocacy and, above all, as is persuading the public. There are always more good ideas than there is money. This is something the public understands instinctively better than many advocates of the single issue.

Politics has its detractors, of course. I want to deal with four major schools: the experts, the business community, the media, and the ideologists of the left and the right.

First, the experts. We know them most evocatively through those wonderful British television programmes, "Yes, Minister" and "Yes, Prime Minister." Some civil servants, as well as the collective expert community both in the universities and outside, frequently take the view that there is one right answer. The right answer is never too hot, never too cold, but is an objective answer that is found by a process, frequently of deductive reasoning. I found in government that there was a certain arrogance on the part of those who felt that they were the permanent government. The politicians who were in the room were really just there by sufferance, here today and gone tomorrow, while the permanent government would go on forever and ever. Administration on its own is a dangerous thing. It has to be led and informed by politics.

The institutions of government themselves need to change. The leadership for this transformation will hardly come from the bureaucracy itself. Governments

have all the problems of any large institutions: hierarchical, always tending to grow in size, seeking to
control more by regulation and an ever-extending
reach. One does not have to embrace all the tenets of
neo-liberal and neo-conservative ideology to recognize that the administrative state brings with it its
own problems and abuses.

Social democrats are troubled by these issues
because there is a such a significant part of our tradition that assumed that "more government" was the
natural answer to so many questions. Fabian reformers were convinced that simply extending the authority of the expert, the scientific rational being with the
objective answer, would solve most social problems.
Most of us today are much more sceptical about the
triumph of this kind of rationality. The administrative
state, taken to extremes, leads to tyranny. On a more
mundane level, it can lead to rigidity, pettifogging
rules, and a political culture that is intolerant of innovation, change, dialogue with the citizenry, and the
existence of other points of view and the other key
elements of civil society.

The experts, then, whether in a public bureaucracy
or in the growing number of consultancies around
the world, provide necessary advice to the process of
making a decision. But expertise has to confront other
views, and the cold bath (or sometimes very hot bath)
of opinion. This has led to the emergence of the
greatest witch doctors of them all, the pollsters. At
their best, and depending on questions asked (and

information provided), pollsters can give you a snapshot of opinion. They can never tell you how it can change. And change it does: we change our minds as individuals, and the public is no different.

Polling is really the classic rear view mirror. It gives an instinctive reaction to what happened in the past. It rarely gives an insight into how people change their minds. Charlottetown was popular in September, 1992. It was toast in six weeks.

The second group of "anti-politics," who are partly connected to those I call the ideologists of the right, are, of course, the businessmen who believe in something called the magic of the market-place, those who advocate a *laissez-faire* philosophy in which their view is "leave everything up to the economy." Economics and business management should be the master sciences, not politics. And again, there is this bogus scientific view that there is an "objective answer" that flows from the natural workings of the market economy and that any attempt to interfere in any way, shape, or form with the magic working of this market-place will lead to disaster. Therefore, in this philosophy, there is nothing for the politician to do except to bow down to the altar of the market-place, to let business do its thing, and for politics to be subservient to the economy and business.

This is an increasingly conventional view. In Ontario, it has become a kind of political orthodoxy. We are told by incantation that everything that happened before the Tories took over in 1995 was bad because it was too "interventionist." Therefore, in this view, we have to revolutionize government, take government completely out of the field of the economy and let the economy do its thing. Like all examples of a conventional wisdom, this excess of business-class logic will eventually pass. But it has already done a great deal of damage.

Of course, the economy in which we live shapes the context in which we practise our politics. It is true that the way our economy works has to be understood. It has become increasingly global. As it becomes increasingly international, we have to focus on what we can do best as governments. Some policy tools will have to be abandoned. Others will need to be taken up. But the idea that the economy itself— or the mere word "globalization"—makes politics irrelevant or meaningless to the human condition is nonsense. It was ideological nonsense when it was put forward by the political economists at the beginning of the nineteenth century and it remains nonsense today.

The dominance of "television culture" has turned politics into a branch of the entertainment industry. If this were not so funny, it would be a serious matter. In *Entertaining Ourselves to Death*, Neil Postman describes the difference between the political and media culture in the U.S. at the time of the American Revolution and today. We could do the same in describing the media at the time of Confederation and media when we tried to reform the constitution in 1991 and 1992 and when previous first ministers and others had to try to reform it in the late 1980s. This phenomenon of politics as entertainment, of news as infotainment, in which it becomes more and more difficult to describe anything to people in clips longer than thirty seconds, in which it is almost impossible to communicate issues requiring thought, reflection, discussion, and debate, is a major problem, because the medium itself defines everything in the context of entertainment.

I see no easy answer to this dilemma. Censorship is not the answer. Neither is more government regulation. A first step is for us to discuss the problem. The power of the media should not go undiscussed or unchallenged. The media investigates and exposes every institution in society except itself. This is a major problem.

To return to our twin reference points, Edmund Burke and George Orwell were both confronting a tide of opinion in favour of one-dimensional, revolutionary answers. Despite their very different perspectives, they shared a sense of what was a reasonable scope for the exercise of political judgement. A space was required for private life, for personal enjoyment, for a boundary to the unbearable intrusiveness of the community which will always interfere unless held back.

We now know that this intrusion takes many forms. The babble of modern television transforms political leaders into figures of fame, whose lives are subjected to the most extraordinary scrutiny. In *1984*, Orwell's hero, Winston Smith, attempted to evade the all-powerful eye of the party in his forbidden relationship with Julia and in his secret meetings with the supposed dissident. The television sets in *1984* could never be turned off. They are scarcely ever turned off today, although this is because of their addictive power instead of a government decree.

The media have now appointed themselves the guardians of the private, as well as public, morality of all those subjected to their gaze. There is a newspeak and doublethink that at first glance is less "political" than the Stalinism of Orwell's day, but in the end is oppressive in its own way. The klieg lights and feeding frenzies have their own special absurdity.

Politicians, in turn, attempt to manipulate the media which control their access to the public. Question period in parliament or the legislature is not about asking questions or giving answers. It is about creating images, impressions, providing headlines, making a sensation. That is as true for the government as it is for the opposition. Cynicism about politics is not exclusively the media's fault. It is deeply ingrained in the public, and indeed always has been. Politicians promise too much and deliver too little. But the media have to take their share of the blame.

I write these words as I watch the central media "events" of our time: Bill Clinton's sex life; the ice storm and its aftermath; Mike Harris's fights with

Mel Lastman and Jean Chrétien; the possibility of another war with Iraq; the issue of Quebec separation being referred to the Supreme Court. All emerge as so much background noise. It is almost impossible to distinguish between fact, rumour, opinion, and pure sensation. Each actor struts his stuff for a brief moment. It is almost impossible to find out how much anthrax Saddam Hussein really has, and what we can realistically expect him to do with it; what Mr. Clinton's private life really has to do with his public responsibilities.

The culture of television has undoubtedly become more trivial and sensational. Dealing with Clinton's problems it becomes harder to tell the difference between the worlds of "Hard Copy," Geraldo Rivera, Jerry Springer, and the six o'clock news. This in turn affects all other outlets, radio and newspapers. The "dumbing down" never stops.

No institution in civil society is as self-righteous or unexamined as the media. Stanley Baldwin, one of Britain's more stolid prime ministers of this century, once scathingly referred to the tabloid press of his day as having "the prerogatives of the harlot through the ages—all power and no responsibility." To talk of accountability is to raise immediately the spectre of censorship or government information review boards, which are impossible to envisage working in practice.

Yet it is hard to imagine that the best we can hope for are hypocritical lectures on sexual morality from commentators whose own lives would never pass the

tests they seek to impose on others, followed by fatuous debates between political extremists revelling in
controversy for its own sake. Most of us don't live our
lives this way. We have conversations, dialogues, questions. We are open to persuasion.

Orwell understood that the abstractions of "propaganda and demotic speech" were designed to obscure
and mislead. Words were twisted against themselves.
Language was used to hide what was actually being
done. We often describe our current political world as
Orwellian because we are swamped by messages from
politicians that are "hyped" and "spun." We are having to teach our children not to believe what they
read and what they hear.

In Orwell's day, the experts at crafting messages
with hidden meaning and buried purpose were the
propagandists of the totalitarian left and right. He
wrote before the image-makers of modern mass marketing were allowed to operate at full throttle on television. Watching the shifting public mood in
response to classic political negative advertising, it is
hard not to recall Orwell's words "hatred can be
turned in any direction at a moment's notice, like a
plumber's blow-flame." This is an insight that Burke
would have understood and agreed with entirely.

What then of the new "revolutionists," the ideologists of the right? What would Burke and Orwell
have made of them? They start from many of the
same premises as Lenin or Robespierre. They have a
theory. They hate the "status quo." Everything that

exists is terrible and must be torn down. Something new and bold will take its place. I have even heard the phrase "you can't make an omelet without breaking eggs" coming from a young Tory staffer, no doubt unaware that this was Lenin's justification for the evils of his revolution. People are not eggs, and all too often an omelet is not the result.

Burke has more in common with modern social democracy than he does with the libertarian excesses of the Progressive Conservative government in Ontario, which is ruling with an almost religious faith in its own "common sense revolution." He believed above all in the sense of mutual obligation that is the heart of community:

> Society is indeed a contract. Subordinate contracts for objects of mere occasional interest may be dissolved at pleasure—but the state ought not to be considered as nothing better than a partnership agreement in a trade of pepper and coffee, calico or tobacco, or some other such low concern, to be taken up for a little temporary interest, and to be dissolved by the fancy of the parties. It is to be looked on with other reverence; because it is a partnership in things subservient only to the gross animal existence of a temporary and perishable nature. It is a partnership in all science; a partnership in all art; a partnership in every virtue, and in all perfection. As the ends of such a partnership cannot be obtained in many generations, it becomes a partnership not only between those who

are living, but between those who are living, those who are dead, and those who are to be born.[4]

· 182 · We need less revolution and more moderation, less a sense of desperate measures and more a sense of steady building. As Burke put it, "You might have repaired those walls; you might have built on those old foundations. You began ill because you began by despising everything that belonged to you."

Both Burke and Orwell shared the perspective that the real condition of the people mattered far more than any theory, that the affirmation of freedom was the critical buttress against the abuse of power, and that leadership and courage were always necessary when conventional opinion lost its way. Important lessons for our own time.

What separates Burke and the contemporary neo-conservative revolutionaries is a profound difference in temperament, a quite different sense in the role of governments and indeed the art of politics itself. In health, education, welfare, and municipal reform, the spirit underlying every proposal from the new right is a contempt for whatever arrangements have been put in place, and a missionary sense that intense sacrifice must be made today for the benefit of generations yet unborn. Burke understood that "perhaps the only moral trust with any certainty in our hands is the care of our own time."

No doubt Burke's instinct for balance and prudence puts him at odds with Orwell's radical sense that old class structures needed to be brought down. But it also separates him from the libertarian impulse that has captured so many right-wing governments. Burke was not a statist by any means. But he understood the importance of a strong civil society, efficient government, and a respect for mutual obligation. Like Orwell, he understood the value of solidarity. So should we all.

The claim of politics is always a relative claim. It is not a road to salvation. There may be such roads, but politics is not among them. It is not the way to eternal truth or to eternal verities. We cannot aspire to this level of certainty. Those who have claimed to be building a heaven on earth have always ended up making it a lot more like hell.

Our twentieth century has been the most violent century in the history of the world. We have a lot to learn from those wise and sage souls, who have reminded each generation of the limits of politics, of the importance of civility and of the need to understand that from this crooked stick, this stick of human nature, nothing straight was ever made. We should not try to make it too straight. Politics is not about perfection. It is about trying to improve lives as they are really, actually lived. As Burke put it, "To improve the life of this generation is already a great task." To this we might add, with Orwell, "Nothing is possible, except to extend the area of sanity little by little."

We need politics because we live in communities and not in complete isolation. A reaffirmation of politics implies a recognition of the community around us. A conservative like Burke was convinced that the revolutionary mindset would eliminate space and civility, as well as the social order to which he was attached. Orwell recognized in the impersonal and bureaucratic forces around him, as well as the technologies over which they had control, a threat to his own sense of private space and civility, although he was hardly attached to the same sense of social order and privilege as Burke. He was, however, attached to a special sense of "Englishness," which made him such a celebrant of the popular culture around him.

We practise our politics in our countries and communities, in our cities and towns, in our offices and places of work, even in our families. The context that shapes this politics changes all the time. But it is a great illusion to believe that we can avoid politics. It adds a necessary substance to our private lives, and indeed gives a broader meaning to our other relationships.

When the economy was expanding and when opportunities appeared to be there for everyone, as they did in the years after the Second World War, we thought that as Canadians we had discovered an extraordinary sense of our own generosity as a people. We spoke with a degree of smugness about how this spirit of generosity was strong in our midst, and how other countries had different traditions. In fact, there is no magic in the Canadian formula. We have discovered that it is harder to expect the same degree of magnanimity in the country in a time of recession and declining economic growth. This doesn't mean that Canadians are bad people or that people have suddenly become less generous. It sim- ply means that in response to a very dramatically changing economic situation people have been inclined, and indeed forced, to look to their own self-interest first and then begin to worry about others. In the course of a caucus discussion one of my NDP colleagues sagely observed that the water buffalo look at one another a little differently as the watering hole dries up.

We are now faced with difficult questions. Do we want to live in cities where there are streets and neighbourhoods where not everyone can go? Do we want to live in communities with rising levels of crime in which the answer to social problems is to incarcerate more and more (and more) people, and build bigger jails? Do we want to live in communities where those who have anything at all have to hire security guards and security dogs and create walled cities and communities around them? Or do we want to live in a community which is strong economically, with healthy markets and a strong sense of innovation and growth but an equally strong commitment to a sense of community health, to equality, and to a sense of inclusion?

Pericles' answer at the beginning of this chapter may help us, which in another context is the simple "Who is my neighbour?" Yet globalization itself makes it more difficult. We know that an important reality of our economy is that there is a significant and powerful minority whose relative share of income and wealth have grown in the last twenty years. Indeed since the mid-1970s Canada has become a more self-interested and a less generous place. Those who are more plugged into the global economy have seen their opportunities and horizons grow. Other Canadians have benefited less, and have a greater sense of falling behind.

It was certainly easier in the old economy, where the role of the nation-state was less ambiguous, to reinforce the logic of community and solidarity. It is harder where elites increasingly feel less connected to the immediate community around them.

Nor is the elite a small group of top-hatted capitalists. This convenient cartoon ignores the broad band of professionals and managers of the digital economy who are the effective voice of the new economy. They are our neighbours too. But they are increasingly disconnected from the immediate communities in which they live. They chafe at high taxes and can't understand the slowness of public bureaucracy, which is in such marked contrast to the technological efficiency of their own workplace. Banks in Canada spend billions on information technology. Hospitals spend millions. Guess which are seen as more efficient and responsive.

The traditional-left answer "public sector good; private sector bad" is as mindless as its right-wing counterpart. Most of us want public institutions that work and a market economy that competes and is innovative.

The left's hang-up with this commonsense obser-
vation is deep-seated, and stems from a long-held view that politics lends itself to more ideological solutions. If the premise of market ideologists is wrong, ideologists of revolution from the left have even more to answer for.

Had Edmund Burke died before 1789, he would be remembered as the boon companion of Charles Fox and Richard Brinsley Sheridan, the scourge of the Tories, the enemy of Warren Hastings, and the intellectual architect of the modern Whig Party. As we all know, this is not what happened. Burke lived to the end of the 1790s, which meant he had to confront the central political question of his day, the French Revolution.

The conventional view among British liberals at the time was that the French Revolution was an event to be supported, even celebrated. An irrational, corrupt *ancien régime* was being replaced. Whatever violence and excesses existed were ultimately less important than the objective of an emerging democracy. Burke insisted that there was nothing liberal or progressive in what was happening in France. He saw in it something sinister: a mass revolution which could only lead in one direction, to an ideological and military dictatorship.

To Burke, those who saw the revolution as part of

the liberal tradition were naïve at best. The events of
1789 to 1793 were not the ultimate expression of
liberalism; they were its very antithesis, in which

ideals of freedom, balance, and civility would all be
sacrificed on an ideological altar of a very different
nature. Burke's Whig contemporaries were appalled
by his reflections. His break with his political friends
of thirty years was profound. He died at the end of
the decade a solitary figure.

Yet looking back now, it is hard not to admire his
insight. His view of events seems even more compelling than, say, that of Thomas Paine, who brought
out his own broadside *The Rights of Man* in response
to Burke. Paine, it is worth recalling, spent months
languishing in a French prison as the revolution took
its vicious course in 1793 and 1794. While Paine's
defence of democracy is eloquent, there is something
more profound in Burke's comment:

> Of this I am certain, that in a democracy, the major-
> ity of the citizens is capable of exercising the most
> cruel oppressions upon the minority, whenever
> strong divisions prevail in that kind of polity, as they
> often must; and that oppression of the minority will
> extend to far greater numbers, and will be carried on
> with much greater fury, than can almost ever be
> apprehended from the dominion of a single sceptre.
> In such a popular persecution, individual sufferers
> are in a much more deplorable condition than in any
> other. Under a cruel prince they have the balmy

compassion of mankind to assuage the smart of their
wounds; they have the plaudits of the people to ani-
mate their generous constancy under their sufferings:
but those who are subjected to wrong under multi-
tudes, are deprived of all external consolation. They
seem deserted by mankind; overpowered by a conspiracy of their whole species.[5]

These last four lines surely point the way to the
central tragedy of the twentieth century, the loss of
life and dignity by millions caught in the web of revolutions, whether of Stalinist or Maoist left or Nazi
right. It is easy to see the parallels with Orwell's ter-
rifying description of totalitarian society in *1984.* The
central figure, Winston Smith, no doubt felt deserted
by mankind, overpowered by a conspiracy of the
whole species.[6]

Burke understood far better than his contemporaries that freedom and revolution are ultimately
incompatible, and that the natural consequence of the
narrow, ideological mindset is the destruction of free
society itself. He also understood that freedom and
order are not incompatible, but are indeed mutually
reinforcing. If order becomes oppressive or irrational,
the answer is to change, to improve, to reform, but
never to destroy or tear down.

Just as Burke was ostracized by his own party for
his insights, so too in our own century Orwell was
pilloried on the left for his "premature" understanding of the despicable tyranny that was Stalinism. He

had difficulty getting his books published. "Paper shortages" was even used as an excuse not to print *Animal Farm.*

Luckily Orwell, like Burke before him, was passionately committed to his own insight, and refused to be silenced or bullied. He ultimately did not care for the orthodoxy of conventional opinion, or the personal cost of political isolation.

Here is Orwell on the ultimate similarity between the objectives of Hitler and Stalin:

> Simply in the interest of efficiency, the Nazis found themselves expropriating, nationalising, destroying the very people they had set out to save. It did not bother them, because their aim was simply power and not any particular form of society. They would just as soon be Reds as Socialists to the tune of anti-Marxist slogans—well and good, smash the Socialists. If the next step is to smash the capitalists to the tune of Marxist slogans—well and good, smash the capitalists. It is all-in wrestling, and the only rule is to win. Russia since 1928 shows distinctly similar reversals of policy, always tending to keep the ruling clique in power. As for the hate-campaigns in which totalitarian regimes ceaselessly indulge, they are real enough while they last, but are simply dictated by the needs of the moment. Jews, Poles, Trotskyists, English, French, Czechs, Democrats, Fascists, Marxists—almost anyone can figure as Public Enemy No 1. Hatred can be turned in any

direction at a moment's notice, like a plumber's blow-flame.[7]

Orwell's commitment to social democracy was not doctrinal. He hated the English class system, unqualified privilege, and the hypocrisy of Empire. He admired solidarity and the practical values of the ordinary citizen. Orwell's final entry in his manuscript notebook is dated 17 April 1949. In it he remarks on hearing English upper-class accents from hospital rooms nearby:

And what voices! A sort of over-fedness, a fatuous self-confidence, a constant bah-bahing of laughter about nothing, above all a sort of heaviness & richness combined with a fundamental ill-will—people who, one instinctively feels, without even being able to see them, are the enemies of anything intelligent or sensitive or beautiful. No wonder everyone hates us so.[10]

He goes on to express a concern about the "greater and ever increasing softness and luxuriousness of modern life" and makes a further comment on the problems facing the Labour government:

The greatest of all the disadvantages under which the left-wing movement suffers: that being a newcomer to the political scene, & having to build itself up out of nothing, it had to create a following by telling lies.

For a left-wing party in power, its most serious antagonist is always its own past propaganda.[8]

The last sentence struck home when I first read it,
and it still does today. The past propaganda of the left,
much of it firmly believed even in the face of experience, is at least as serious an antagonist to the successes and fortunes of the New Democratic Party as
any opposition from the right, just as the most difficult issues facing the Chrétien government have been
its own promises and its inability to keep them.

Social democracy has to come to terms with two
issues. The first is whether the vision of the party
implies at all a complete break with the market economy of self-interested individuals and companies in
favour of common ownership and planning. The second is perhaps more mundane, but equally important:
how the party's behaviour and rhetoric in opposition
have created a mentality that is incompatible with the
choices inherent in governing.

Nothing in the experience of social democracy in
Canada or other countries would lead one to think
that these questions are insurmountable. Indeed they
have been resolved in almost every social democratic
party. But their resolution in Canada has not been as
emphatic and clear as it needs to be.

The general commitment among social democratic
parties to the mixed economy which included private
capital was set by the 1950s, but it still stirs the odd-
est of debates. Any political party which does not

appreciate that private entrepreneurship represents a critical and necessary feature of a modern economy deserves to disappear. The Orwell of the years after 1936 might disagree, but on this point he is romantic and unhelpful.

Which leads to my second point. Pierre Trudeau's observation that powerlessness corrupts is accurate. Where social democracy has been most successful in Canada, in the province of Saskatchewan, it has run balanced budgets, cut debt, trimmed bureaucracy, and ultimately, lowered taxes (once these objectives had been achieved). It has also pioneered social and economic reform to reinforce solidarity and strengthen community. A prolonged proximity to power has fostered a sense of timing, patience, and discipline which are entirely admirable.

Prolonged opposition breeds a climate of promise-making, resolution-passing, self-righteous tendentiousness which runs completely contrary to the needs of any governing party. It has allowed the party to wallow in the rhetoric of being a "conscience," as if this was what politics was all about. Politics is about the persuasion required to move people to judgement.

Judgement is by definition a matter of choosing between alternatives, none of which may at any given time be desirable. Is there really only one "moral" response to a dictator sitting on a supply of anthrax? Is it more or less moral to borrow money to fund a social investment? Or is it more moral to lower the deficit and eventually allow more room for spending on education and health care? The premise that questions of political choice lend themselves to one ethical answer is an enduring residue of fundamentalist thinking that has little to do with reality.

A successful social democratic party will despise neither prosperity nor power. It will respect markets and businesses. It will admire innovation, hard work, and education. It will fight for a sustainable economy, for equality, and for solidarity, but will understand that none of these can be achieved with an excess of partisanship. We must understand the priority of politics, but also appreciate its limits.

If Not Now, When?

LIFE IS NOT A REHEARSAL. JUST AS WE FIND excuses for delay in our own lives, putting difficult decisions aside can become habit-forming in politics as well. It is easier to stick with old habits and traditional arguments long after they have ceased to apply or even make sense.

The pursuit of self-interest is a healthy and natural start to public life, just as it is to our own psychic health. Rabbi Hillel's first question is an expression of this pragmatic sense that there is little point (and indeed much potential for tyranny) in denying people's primary desire to improve their own lives. This urge to self-expression, this quest for dignity and recognition for our own worth, whether as individuals or communities, is as fundamental to understanding politics as it is to much else.

Social democracy's origins can be traced to this innate impulse, since it really stemmed from a keen sense that power structures that denied legitimacy to working people, to blacks and other minorities, or to women and their assertion of identity had to be challenged and changed. Just as liberalism insisted on the need to change old structures because they provided no way for self-interest to be reflected or expressed, democratic arguments about extending the franchise, dissolving colonial ties and the embrace of the imperial idea, and finding real room for ordinary people have become an undeniable part of what we see as the basis of a good society.

Capitalism and democracy have long lived in an accommodation in most Western countries. It is an accommodation that only works when balances are struck. There have been several moments when the social contract has come perilously close to the breaking point. In the nineteenth century the gap between rich and poor seemed so large that social movements arose which insisted that the condition of the people was at least as great a question as the primacy of property and the free market.

Efforts were made to bring the "robber barons" and the "malefactors of great wealth" to heel—social insurance schemes were devised, competition laws were passed. Even the U.S. Congress decreed in 1916 that "labour is not a commodity."

The thirties saw the next great round of reform as the Depression shook the system to its roots. Some in the plutocracy of the day saw Roosevelt as a Red and a revolutionary. The more enlightened realized he was someone who believed in democracy, enterprise, and government, and saw nothing contradictory in this faith. Burke would have understood him because he believed in reform in order to preserve. The modern welfare-state reforms that we associate with Roosevelt were consolidated and improved in virtually every Western country until the 1970s. The failure to introduce comprehensive health care in the United States has left the U.S. shortchanged.

A very different set of economic and political circumstances today leaves us with our own great challenge. The reforms of Lloyd George or Roosevelt were premised on national economies and nation-states. No one doubted or challenged the premise, although many differed with the policies put forward.

Hillel's second question can no longer be answered only in a local context. The mobility of capital, its global reach, has now reached the point where democracy and the state have greater difficulty intervening and responding. Some argue that this should be met by governments simply taking up the old tools. Controls on foreign exchange, capital flows, more public ownership, higher tariffs: in short, more protection and intervention.

It would be wrong to dismiss these approaches. There are certainly times, for example, when Canadian industry quite rightly invokes anti-dumping laws to ensure that competition with foreign producers remains fair. But it is hard to see a deeply protec-

tionist strategy as having much long-term appeal. Mobility is a highly prized value, as is choice. Consumers want to be able to choose from a wide variety of products, no matter where they are produced, at the lowest possible price. They do not want the state telling them what they can buy and where they can put their money.

Governments and democracies are not impotent. Nor are they omnipotent. Our challenge now is to create a politics that can reassert its relationship to the real economy. That means more co-operation and co-ordination with other countries, more international rules that are based on more than just the convenience of capital. The trouble with the Multilateral Agreement on Investment is that it ignores the problem of the democratic deficit, and belittles the legitimacy of politics. It is also unnecessary.

Americans are rightly preoccupied with the dramatic decline of the inner city, and the sheer weight of the damage caused by a culture of violence, substance abuse, and crime. As Canadians we like to think of ourselves as superior to these problems. Yet the same economy can produce the same trends: there are native ghettos in our own cities that will only too quickly rival the tragedy of inner Chicago and Detroit. We shall have trouble admitting it to ourselves, but it is true nonetheless. Unless work is found and education takes hold as the central value, poverty will take an even deeper hold of the next generation: then we shall reap the whirlwind.

The extraordinary silence which greeted the Royal Commission on Aboriginal Peoples (1997) is a sure sign of the depth of the denial on the part of too many Canadians. No doubt the media focus on the price tag associated with a myriad of programmes and initiatives (misleadingly high because anything would have to be done over a multi-year timetable) was impossible to absorb in the context of reduced government spending everywhere else.

Yet it is hard to know how the status quo, or even a gentle modification of it, will really begin to address the problem we face. When race and systemic inequality are mixed together, the result is always explosive. Sometimes the explosions happen inside one unhappy soul—the statistics on suicide and family violence are only too eloquent an expression of that—but unless we act we shall all be touched.

What kind of action? Anything that focuses on mutual respect and recognition, education, and work. A people needs a voice. A people needs its own politics. A community of interest naturally seeks its own self-expression. This does not mean every native band council becomes its own country. It does mean the issue of political representation must be addressed.

The inner cities of London and Paris are a reminder that the offspring of their empires have come home. What we find in Winnipeg and Regina is that our colonization was even closer. We cannot escape our history.

Social democracy must change so that it can once again become a healthy and realistic public philosophy. We should be setting stronger rules for markets, and recognizing that while not everything is for sale, innovation, technological change and the fundamental importance of education have everything to do with the creation of wealth. We should not be ashamed of seeking prosperity.

But a prosperity that is too confined and exclusive begins to take on its own pathology. The rich hardly give away enough money to make up for the relative decline in tax revenues and government expenditure. This means poorer schools, a weakened health-care system, and social services for children and the vulnerable that have gone from barely adequate to impoverished.

If the rising tide fails to lift all boats, resentments will increase. Sometimes these resentments will find their expression in too much nationalism, in resistance to immigration, in gender wars, or in varieties of religious fanaticism. Often they find a home in a climate of public mean-spiritedness that appeals to our baser instincts.

It does not have to be this way. It is possible to admit the legitimate claims of prosperity without abandoning the commitment to the public good. The right is talking unity. A broad social democratic and liberal left should be doing the same. Unless this happens, the right will establish its dominance over programmes and ideas, and then (as in Ontario) government itself.

More than a hundred years ago, progressives alarmed at the brutality of the industrial revolution insisted on the need for balance, and on the role of unions, communities, and the state as a necessary countervail to private monopoly. In the middle of our own revolution, we need the same insight: the difficulty is that government itself needs to change, and the bounds of the nation-state are too narrow to balance what has gone wrong.

The democratic spirit can be a great force. We need more of it to give hope to those who feel abandoned and bewildered in this brave new world of rapid change.

ENDNOTES

CHAPTER 1

1. Margaret Fairley, ed. *The Selected Writings of William Lyon Mackenzie* (Toronto: McClelland & Stewart, 1960), 8.

CHAPTER 2

1. George Grant, *Lament for a Nation* (Toronto: McClelland & Stewart, 1965), 4.
2. Ibid., 90.
3. John Locke, "Labour," 1693; from his *Common Place Book* in John Locke, *Political Writings* (London: Penguin, 1993), 440.
4. Karl Marx, *Communist Manifesto, 1848*, in Karl Marx *The Revolutions of 1848: Political Writings*, Vol. 1 (London: Secker & Warburg, 1968), 94.

5. George Orwell, *The Collected Essays, Journalism and Letters*, Vol. 4 (London: Secker & Warburg, 1968), 94.

6. Ibid., Vol. 3, 294.

7. John Kenneth Galbraith, *The Good Society* (Boston/New York: Houghton Mifflin Company, 1996), 117–118.

CHAPTER 3

1. Susan Strange, *The Retreat of the State* (New York: Cambridge University Press, 1996), 8.

2. Ibid., 193.

3. Francis Fukuyama, *The End of History and the Last Man* (New York: Free Press, 1992); and *Trust* (New York: Free Press, 1996).

CHAPTER 4

1. See especially "The Myth of the Powerless State," *The Economist*, October 7, 1995, 15–16 and "The Future of the State," *The Economist*, September 20, 1997, S5.

2. See among other places, *The Economist*, May 31, 1997.

3. Robert Skidelsky, *After Communism* (London: Macmillan, 1993).

4. Galbraith, op. cit., 50.

5. OFL, *The Ontario Alternative Budget Papers* (Toronto: James Lorimer, 1997), 23.

CHAPTER 5

1. Sidney and Beatrice Webb, *The English Poor Law, a History*, Vol. 2 (London: Frank Cass & Co., 1963 reprint), 62.

2. Ibid., 18.

3. John Richards, *Retooling the Welfare State* (Toronto: C.D. Howe Institute, c. 1997).

CHAPTER 6

1. *Time*, February 3, 1997.

2. *Entropy*, 1997, 6.

CHAPTER 7

1. McGee's speech on federalism in the Confederation Debates is a classic. Peter Waite, ed., *The Confedertion Debates* (Toronto: McClelland & Stewart, 1963).

2. See Gerald Craig, ed., *Lord Durham's Report* (Toronto: McClelland & Stewart, c. 1968), 148.

3. Ibid., 149.

4. Baldwin's speech can be found in George Locke, ed., *Builders of the Canadian Commonwealth* (Toronto: Ryerson Press, 1923), 27. On the friendship between Baldwin and Lafontaine see John Ralston Saul, *Reflections of a Siamese Twin* (Toronto: Viking, 1997).

5. Lafontaine's speech is in Waite, op. cit., 41.

6. Macdonald's letter is quoted in Peter Waite, *The Life and Times at Confederation* (Toronto: University of Toronto Press, 1962), 123.

7. Taché's speech is in Peter Waite, *The Confederation Debates*, op. cit., 127.

8. W.P.M. Kennedy, *The Canadian Constitution* (Toronto: Oxford University Press, 1931), 406–407.

9. Charles Handy, *The Age of Paradox* (Boston: Harvard University Press, 1995), 110.

10. Ibid., 112.

11. All quotations are from *Reference re Secession of Quebec* [1998] S.C.J. no. 61.

12. Royal Commission on Bilingualism and Biculturalism, *Report* (Ottawa: Queen's Printer, 1965), 133.

13. Ibid., 106.

14. Ibid., 170.

CHAPTER 8

1. Thucydides, *The Peloponnesian War*, Richard Crawley (1874) revised for *The Landmark Thucydides*, ed. Robert B. Strassler (New York: Free Press, 1996), 148.

2. All of Orwell's books are conveniently reprinted by Penguin Books. There are three good biographies of Orwell: Bernard Crick, *George Orwell: A Life* (London: Secker & Warburg, 1980); Michael Shelden, *Orwell, The Authorized Biography* (London: Heinemann, 1991); George Woodcock, *The Crystal Spirit* (Boston: Little, Brown, 1966).

3. See John Morley, *Burke* (London: Macmillan and Co., 1909), 54.

4. Edmund Burke, *Reflections on the Revolution in France* (London: Penguin, 1968), 194–195. Conor Cruise O'Brien's book *Edmund Burke* (London: Sinclair-Stevenson, 1997) is the best introduction.

5. Burke, *Reflections*, 121.

6. George Orwell, *1984* (London: Penguin, 1954), 117.

7. George Orwell, *The Collected Essays, Journalism and Letters*, Vol. 4 (London: Secker & Warburg, 1968), 515.

8. Ibid., 515.